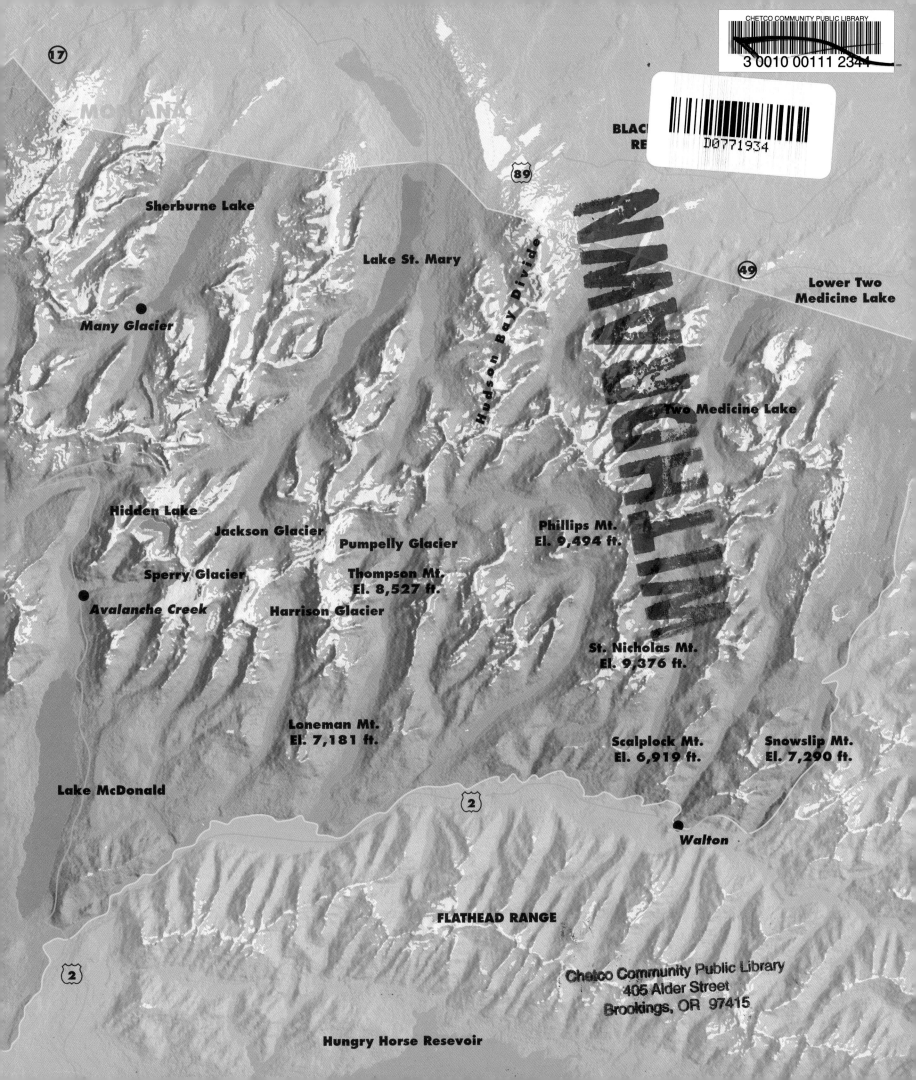

⑰

MONTANA

Sherburne Lake

Lake St. Mary

89

BLACK
RE

49

Lower Two
Medicine Lake

Many Glacier

Hudson Bay Divide

MONTANA

Two Medicine Lake

Hidden Lake

Jackson Glacier

Pumpelly Glacier

Phillips Mt.
El. 9,494 ft.

Sperry Glacier

Thompson Mt.
El. 8,527 ft.

Avalanche Creek

Harrison Glacier

St. Nicholas Mt.
El. 9,376 ft.

Loneman Mt.
El. 7,181 ft.

Scalplock Mt.
El. 6,919 ft.

Snowslip Mt.
El. 7,290 ft.

Lake McDonald

2

Walton

FLATHEAD RANGE

2

Hungry Horse Resevoir

"When I have to describe Glacier to someone who hasn't been there . . . my mouth trips over inadequate adjectives. The magic of it never leaves me, but when I'm not there I'm haunted by the insufficiency of my memory to do it justice."

PAUL SCHULLERY

GLACIER &

LAND OF HANG

PAUL

PHOTOGRAPHY

HarperCollins*SanFrancisco* *A Division of* HarperCollins*Publishers*

WATERTON

ING VALLEYS

SCHULLERY

BY JEFF GARTON

A Tehabi Book

Page 1:

Avalanche Creek's noisy rush down a narrow gorge has sculpted and polished the argillite bedrock into a series of moss-draped bowls and pockets, easily enjoyed from the Avalanche Lake Trail.

Pages 2-3:

Early autumn snows on Red Eagle Peak in eastern Glacier National Park.

Pages 4-5:

The meadows of Hanging Gardens, near Logan Pass, with the storm-obscured Garden Wall in the distance.

Pages 6-7:

Glacier's rocky terrain climbs up from one rugged, amphitheater-like cirque and down into another, this one below Heavy Runner and Reynolds Mountains.

Pages 8-9:

Dawn begins the daily light show at St. Mary Lake.

The Genesis Series was conceived by Tehabi Books and published by Harper Collins San Francisco. The series celebrates the epic geologic processes that created and continue to shape America's magnificent national parks and their distinctive ecosystems. Each book is written by one of the nation's most evocative nature writers and features images from some of the best nature photographers in the world.

Glacier & Waterton: Land of Hanging Valleys was conceived and produced by Tehabi Books, Del Mar, California. Nancy Cash–*Managing Editor*; Andy Lewis–*Art Director*; Sam Lewis–*Art Director*; Tom Lewis–*Editorial and Design Director*; Sharon Lewis–*Controller*; Chris Capen–*President*. Additional support for *Glacier & Waterton: Land of Hanging Valleys* was provided by Susan Wels–*Series Editor*; Jeff Cambell–*Copy Editor*; Anne Hayes–*Copy Proofer*.

Written by Paul Schullery, *Glacier & Waterton: Land of Hanging Valleys* features the photography of Jeff Garton. Supplemental photography was provided by Carl Mondragon (pgs. 91, 96, 98, 108) and Tom and Pat Leeson (pg. 86). Technical, 3-D illustrations were produced by Sam Lewis. Source materials for the illustrations were provided as digital elevation models from the United States Geological Survey. Additional illustrations were produced by Andy Lewis and Tom Lewis.

For more information on Waterton/Glacier International Peace Park, Harper Collins San Francisco and Tehabi Books encourage readers to contact the Glacier Natural History Association, P.O. Box 428, West Glacier MT 59936; (406) 888-5756.

Harper Collins San Francisco and Tehabi Books, in association with The Basic Foundation, a not-for-profit organization whose primary mission is reforestation, will facilitate the planting of two trees for every one used in the manufacture of this book.

Library of Congress Cataloging-in-Publication Data
Schullery, Paul
    Glacier & Waterton: Land of Hanging Valleys / Paul Schullery:
  photography by Jeff Garton.
        p. cm.—(The Genesis Series)
    "A Tehabi Book"
    Includes index.
    ISBN 0-06-258568-1 (cloth).—ISBN 0-06-258563-0 (pbk.).
    1. Glacier National Park (Mont.) 2. Glacier National Park (Mont.)—Pictorial works.
    3. Waterton Lakes National Park (Alta.) 4. Waterton Lakes National Park (Alta.)—Pictorial works
    I. Garton, Jeff. II. Title. III. Series: Genesis Series.
    F737.G5S39 1996
    978.6'52—dc20   95-47252
                                                            CIP

96 97 98 99 TBI 10 9 8 7 6 5 4 3 2 1

This edition is printed on acid-free paper that meets the American National Standards Institute Z39.48 Standard.

THE GENESIS SERIES

GLACIER & WATERTON

LAND OF HANGING VALLEYS

I first saw Waterton and Glacier National Parks in the early 1970s as a young man traveling cheap in a world of fresh wonders. With no effort, I can still recall a remarkable number of moments from that first visit. Some were bare impressions, but they stuck and still form my mental image of the place: a combination of landscape and skyscape, the peaks holding violent weather like towering, dark ephemeral ridges atop the more substantial stone ones.

Other moments were small revelations of natural history: I first saw a dipper, perhaps my favorite bird, "fly" underwater at Avalanche Lake. I got my first close look at a blue grouse by a rock wall on Going-to-the-Sun Road.

Other recollections usually only come back to me when I return to their source. There's a little wetland not far from Apgar where I saw a moose, and though I've never seen another one there since, I still pass it with the reflexive thought, "Here's a good place for moose."

Other memories are perhaps just weird. One night at Sprague Creek Campground, I "camped" in my little car, the passenger side of which I'd converted into a bunk. That night the car was apparently a trifle tilted, with my head lower than my feet and aimed toward the lake. In the middle of the night I awoke from a terrifying nightmare of my car coasting back into the dark water. This memory is firmly enshrined in my personal Hall of Great Moments of Panic. I remember a black bear near Coppermine Creek, a field of pale paintbrush near Camas Creek Entrance Station, road-side mule deer

OF BEGINNINGS

Snowmelt from the 9,642-foot Going-to-the-Sun Mountain waters the lush slopes below.

begging for handouts, and all the unforgettable and almost unbelievable views one gets even without stopping the car. At the time I was hopelessly hooked on the magic of another mountain landscape—Yellowstone—but I knew immediately that this place was also worth a lifetime of attention and passion.

A few years earlier, when I first applied for work as a seasonal park ranger, I was asked to fill out a form listing my preferred choices among the parks. It amuses me to remember that I put Glacier down as my first choice and Yellowstone second, though I have never regretted for a minute that I was hired by Yellowstone. At the time I'd only been to Yellowstone twice and had never even seen Glacier, but somehow it just sounded better, perhaps because I imagined it would be less crowded. I can't even imagine how the years would have gone if Glacier had hired me rather than Yellowstone, but I imagine that Glacier would have given me just as good a start. It is, after all, very good at starting things.

Amid the jumble of peaks along the east side of Glacier National Park stands one that, though neither the tallest nor the most photogenic, must certainly be the most symbolic. At barely eight thousand feet, Triple Divide Peak is lower than many of its neighbors, but a quirk of geography distinguishes it from the rest, for it is the central dividing point for all of North America. Rain and snowmelt run down its western slopes into Pacific Creek, from there into Nyack Creek and on out of the park, eventually to the Pacific Ocean. Water draining the east side of Triple Divide becomes Atlantic Creek, which flows into Cut Bank Creek, which leaves the park on its way to the Gulf of Mexico. Water running to the north creates Hudson Bay Creek, whose ultimate destination is given away by its name. The great naturalist and conservationist George Bird Grinnell didn't have to know about Triple Divide Peak in order to justify calling this region "The Crown of the Continent," but this one peak clinches the case beyond all doubt. Many things begin here.

An appreciation for the rooflike nature of this country existed long before Grinnell published his famous "Crown of the Continent" article in *Century* magazine in 1901. The ancestors of the people now living on the Blackfeet Indian Reservation, which borders Glacier National Park on the east, called these mountains "the Backbone."

In some ways, the two thousand or so square miles of Waterton and Glacier National Parks have changed a lot since those names were applied, but most of the changes have been administrative; they show on the maps but they don't show at all on the land. Waterton was first set aside as a forest reserve in 1895, and Glacier became a national park in 1910. In 1932, in a profound and enduring gesture of good will, the two were combined as Waterton/Glacier International Peace Park. That too was the beginning of many good things.

Like many of the park's cirques, Avalanche Lake's drains the higher country through wispy, undulating cascades so long that they might be thought of as vertical creeks.

FOLLOWING PAGES:

Fed by Sexton Glacier and snow fields between Going-to-the-Sun Mountain and Matahpi Peak, Baring Creek tumbles and splashes on its way to St. Mary Lake.

About dusk, small rainbow trout began rising here and there thirty or forty yards out from the lakeshore. Though I much prefer stream fishing to lake fishing (it would amaze the uninitiated how snooty fly fishermen can be about where they'll bother to fish, even with feeding trout in sight), I'd brought a rod and a "light vest" (read "a vest with only a couple hundred flies in it") and wanted to give it a try. On a stream, I'll usually bother to study the situation a little, but on a lake, I just tie on some general, hopeful, big fly and start slapping it out there, wishing for this to be a night the fish don't care what I offer. What the hell, they're just little rainbows in a wilderness lake—how smart can they be?

Of course they usually do care, and they can be very smart. My line had a heavy leader tippet, but I didn't want to bother putting on a finer one that would be less obvious to the fish, so I sloshed out into the shallows and started casting.

It was immediately clear that I needed more than the right fly. What I really needed were chest waders, preferably insulated chest waders, or even a boat. I was wading in shorts, and I'd borrowed Marsha's rubber sandals, which were about two inches too short for my feet; my heels overhung them and kept coming down on sharp rocks, so I accompanied my casting with a refrain of "Ooch, ouch, ooch" as I waded along. Worse, every time I laid that heavy leader and big fly out over a riser, the fish immediately fled the area.

THREE CIRQUES

NOTES FROM THE GREAT DIVIDE

For a while I thought that my only consolation would be the glorious view. Steep, raw ridges with dark, twisted strata ran up in various directions, towering more than two thousand feet above the lake on three sides and reflected hugely in the water. But then, as so often happens when I start fishing lazily and without thought, I recalled that I do know how to fish, and I became engaged in the game. Up to my waist and shivering in the cold lake, I used what was left of the light to improve my gear, experimenting with smaller and smaller flies, tip-toeing into deeper spots to make longer casts, and through a combination of contortions and grunts generally managing to keep my backcasts out of the tall willows that lined the shore.

Just as my feet began to go numb and it got too dark to pick another fly from the box, I attached a three-foot section of very fine tippet material to my leader, tied on a tiny Quill Gordon (a #20, for you fishermen) and put it over another riser. The fish rose confidently, took it, and was hooked. Uttering a loud and triumphant "Ha!" I hauled back on the rod like a tuna fisherman landing an eighty-pounder, the leader parted well above the fly, and my fish was gone.

It is another part of the perversity of fly fishing that one can feel so successful without having landed a fish. Having now figured out the situation, and having proven it by hooking a trout, I didn't need to continue. Oh, I made some more casts, but I soon went back to the tent in search of some warm socks and maybe a little wine.

Gunsight Goats

Gunsight Lake occupies a mile-long trough at the bottom of a more or less east-facing cirque that drains northeast from the park and eventually into Hudson Bay. From the lake it's a three-mile climb and a 1,600-foot elevation change to Gunsight Pass and the Continental Divide. There were nine of us in the group: Marsha and I in one tent; Jeremy, Wendy, and their three-year-old daughter Kessie in another tent; and Miles, Zerc, Pinball, and Petey, our rent-a-llamas, over by the hitching post. We'd made the six-mile hike from the Going-to-the-Sun Road that day, and while I fished, the others tidied up the cooking gear, hung our bright red llama-panniers to keep them out of reach of bears and deer, and generally got comfortable for the night.

It had been a very dry August, and there were some big fires west of the park; in fact, it was so dry that the national forests out there were closed to hiking. But the only effect it had on us was to make all the views hazy and the predawn skies a deep rose. On such a dawn, after two cool nights camped at the shore of the lake, we rammed everything back in the panniers, hung them on the sides of the llamas, and marched off to conquer the pass. After the rest of us crossed the swaying footbridge across the outlet of the lake, Marsha (wearing her own sandals now) led the four llamas across the shallow stream, and we began to climb.

The trail to Gunsight Lake winds past marshy Mirror Lake, with ice-patched Mount Jackson looming in the distance.

FOLLOWING PAGES:

On a still dawn, Gunsight Lake mirrors the surrounding slopes and the distant notch of Gunsight Pass.

THE SYMBOLIC GOAT

Much more than the grizzly, the mountain goat has been the traditional symbol of Glacier National Park. The Great Northern Railway, which had so much to do with the opening of Glacier to visitors in its early years, adopted the goat as its symbol, and a more admirable one is hard to imagine. There is no precise count of Glacier's goats, but they seem to number more than 1,400, so your chance of seeing one is excellent, whether you hike into the backcountry or just stick to the roads. Once you see them in action on the slopes (rather than licking up tasty radiator antifreeze in the parking lot at Logan Pass), you'll immediately appreciate why they inspire such awe. A band of goats picking its way across some nearly sheer cliff face can evoke as much disbelief as empathetic nervousness. In his milestone book A Beast the Color of Winter: The Mountain Goat Observed, *some of which was based on the author's research in Glacier,* Douglas Chadwick describes how the goat's exceptional traction and tremendous chest and shoulder muscles allow it to move around: "I have seen mountain goats perform what amounted to one-handed chin-ups. Having only a scrap of momentum behind them they reached out, hooked one hoof on an overhead shelf, and hauled themselves up by it alone." So, while it's wonderful to see one along a road, the real treat is seeing one, even at a great distance, on one of the high steep places where they make their home.

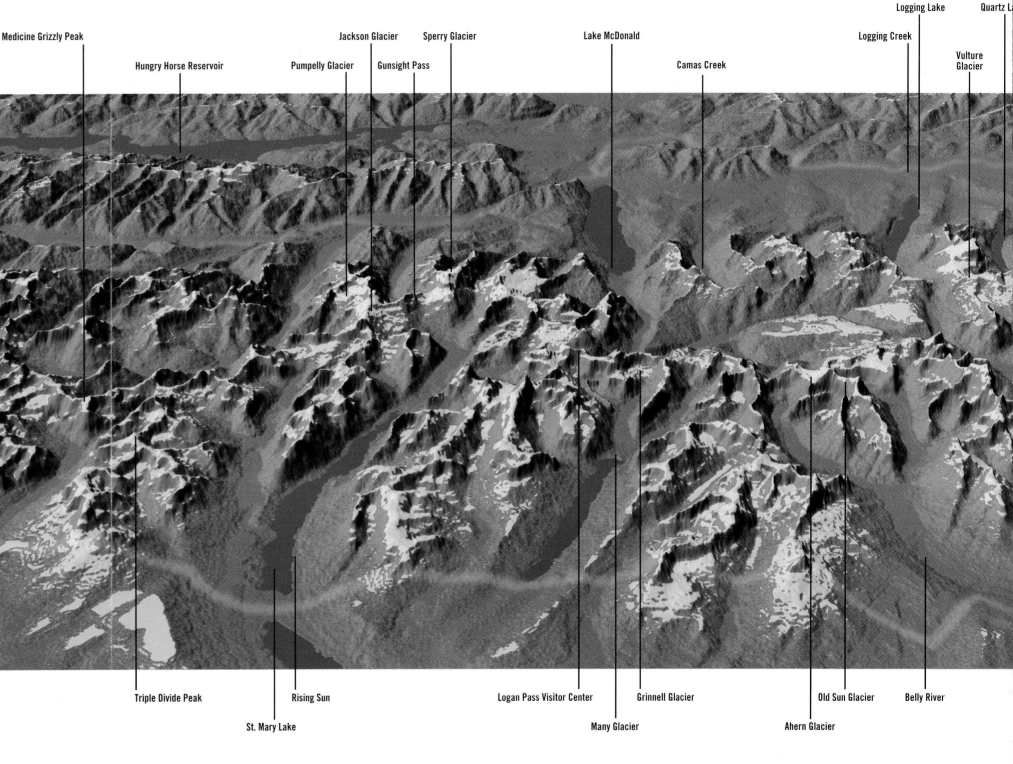

topographic divides defines something essential about the continent's character, and a topographically minded person standing anywhere downstream in any of these drainages will look to this point more than any other as the place where it begins.

More than half of Glacier National Park drains west, part of the Columbia River Basin. The entire western boundary of the park is defined by running water—the North and Middle Forks of the mighty Flathead River. All water flowing out this side of the park drains away from the boundary at one point, a few miles west of the West Entrance.

The southeast corner of the park yields the flows of Cut Bank, Two Medicine, and other small creeks. These almost immediately become slow, meandering prairie streams, making their way to the Missouri River, which drains so much of Montana.

The northeast section of Glacier Park and all of Waterton Lakes Park gather nearly all their flow in three main rivers: St. Mary, emerging from the largest lake chains on the east side of Glacier Park; Belly River, a hemmed-in system draining a number of smaller (but no less glorious) lakes near the Canadian border; and Waterton, a drainage with almost as much acreage in the U.S. park as in the Canadian one. All three trend to the northeast, large prairie rivers with a long way to go to Hudson Bay.

Labels on the image:

Weasel Colla Glacier
Logging Lake
Quartz L
Lower Two Medicine Lake
Medicine Grizzly Peak
Jackson Glacier
Sperry Glacier
Lake McDonald
Logging Creek
Two Medicine Lake
Walton
Hungry Horse Reservoir
Pumpelly Glacier
Gunsight Pass
Camas Creek
Vulture Glacier
Triple Divide Peak
Rising Sun
Logan Pass Visitor Center
Grinnell Glacier
Old Sun Glacier
Belly River
St. Mary Lake
Many Glacier
Ahern Glacier

I'd never encountered an animal before that seemed to enjoy a good view the way the llamas did. Whenever we stopped at a steep place, my llama, Miles, would move right to the edge and gaze intently off into the smoky distance. I suppose a few thousand generations of South American mountain lions made them that way.

They were terrific animals to hike with. They were cooperative, attentive, and enormously amusing, and their habit of humming back and forth to each other was a soothing force I missed for weeks after the trip was over. But nobody had prepared them for goats. This was all the more surprising because they barely deigned to notice the deer we encountered on the trail and at the Gunsight Lake campsite.

Gunsight Pass's goats, a little like the goats at Logan Pass on Going-to-the-Sun Road, are famous. Because of their "habituation" to people (which makes them both a management problem and easy to study) they've been the subject of repeated research projects, and we'd been assured we'd have no trouble seeing them. Sad to say, neither did the llamas. We'd stopped for a break about three-quarters of the way to the pass when Miles and Zerc, the two lead llamas, became intent on a distant white object high on the slope above us. Zerc suddenly let loose with the llama's alarm call, a sound much like a turkey would make if it weighed about four hundred pounds, a sound so loud that you don't want to be standing directly by the llama's mouth (as Marsha was) when it makes it. The goat eventually disappeared behind a low ridge, and we packed up our water bottles and headed on up the trail. I was leading Miles, with Marsha right behind me with Zerc, followed by Wendy leading Pinball and Petey strung together.

A minute later, I led Miles around a sharp turn in the trail and was suddenly confronted with a nanny and kid goat only twenty feet away. Miles bolted in a panic, leaving the trail and scrambling back downhill across a steep, rocky meadow, dragging panniers, packs, and—until I had the good sense to let go of his rope—me. Though I was too busy to notice, Zerc had done the same thing (Marsha did have the good sense to let go right away). At first I thought they were planning to retreat a long way down the mountain, and I was at least grateful that this hadn't happened on one of the narrow places where the only choices are back down the trail or over the edge. But all they wanted to do was get with the other llamas. As soon as all four were standing side by side in a row, facing the perceived threat, they no longer wanted to run.

It took a while to get going again. We had to hold the llamas' reins very tight while the two goats bypassed us and moved down the trail, then we had to make sure none of us had broken anything before restoring Miles's panniers. Miles was only bleeding a little from one leg, and my twisted ankle hardly hurt at all. From then on, for the next couple days, whenever we were hiking a steep, winding trail, I could look back and see all four llamas craning their necks as far out to one side as possible in order to see what sort of bizarre surprise we might spring on them next.

TOPOGRAPHY OF GLACIER & WATERTON

The Continental Divide snakes through the western mountains the length of North America, turning this way and that in response to local drainage quirks, but always honoring the call of gravity. In Glacier National Park, at Triple Divide Peak, it meets another divide, the one between the Hudson Bay drainage and the Gulf of Mexico drainage. This second divide, though easy to follow on park maps, becomes a very subtle feature of the landscape out on the Great Plains east of the park; the separation between the Missouri River Basin and the drainages to the north is defined not by towering peaks but by rolling prairie, where the passing motorist is unlikely to realize that some feature of continental significance has just been crossed.

Glacier & Waterton is a geographical starting point, but it must be remembered that this is in good part a symbolic beginning. It isn't as if Triple Divide Peak is the only headwaters for all streams flowing into Hudson Bay, or the Gulf of Mexico, or the Pacific Ocean. The entire lengths of both the Continental Divide and the Hudson Bay Divide are headwaters, so countless little streams beginning hundreds and even thousands of miles from Triple Divide contribute to the flow as well.

On the other hand, the symbolism of the "Crown of the Continent" is profound. The meeting of these

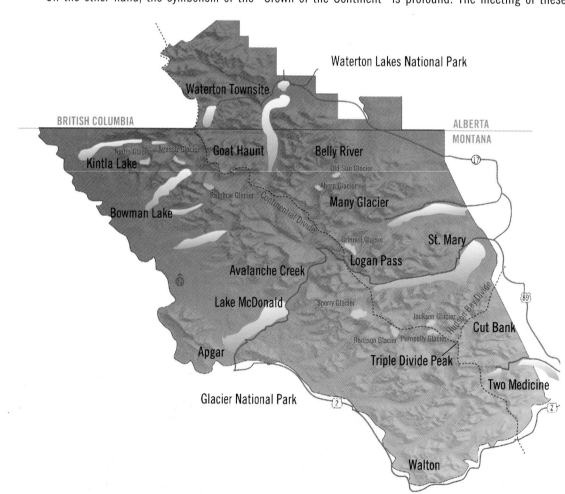

nbow Glacier

Bowman Lake

Thunderbird Glacier   Agassiz Glacier

Kintla Glacier   Kintla Lake

Goat Haunt   Waterton Lake   Mount Crandell

Waterton Townsite

The "Crown of the Continent" concept does, of course, ignore large parts of North America not drained from these divides: all the rivers flowing to the Arctic Ocean, the entire Atlantic seaboard, the drainages of countless Pacific Coastal range streams, and so on. But again, the symbolism holds because the magnitude of what starts at Triple Divide Peak is sufficient to support it. The water runs from this place, taking with it the materials to build new sediments in faraway oceans that may themselves someday become dry and rise to be carved into equally magnificent landscapes in some vastly distant future.

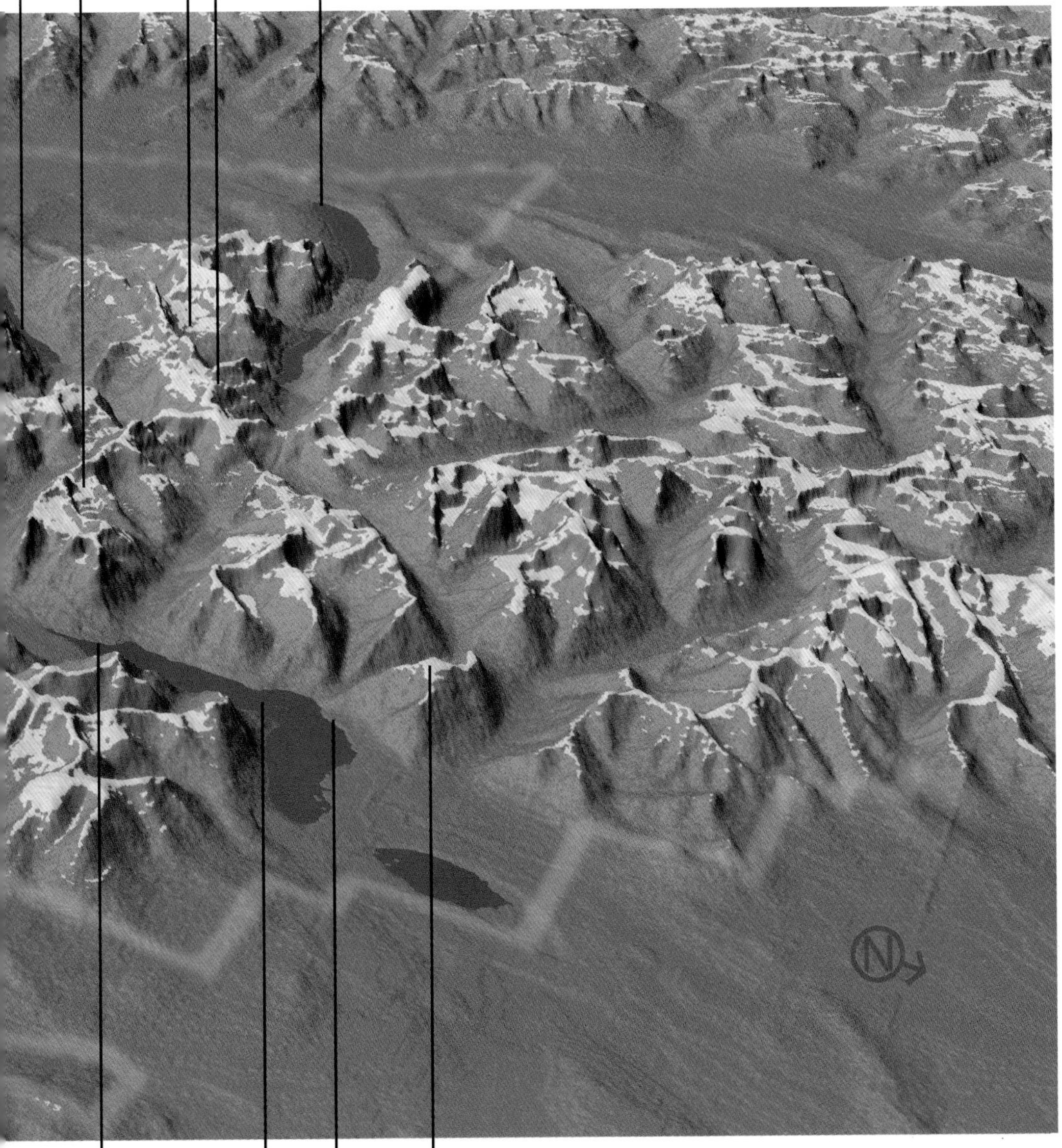

Note: Although it may look like a photograph, this image is actually a computerized, extruded, topographic view. It was created using digital elevation models derived from the United States Geological Survey (USGS) satellite maps and traditional, flat USGS topographic maps.

To prepare the extruded topo map, data from the USGS was downloaded from the Earth Science Information Center to a personal computer and converted into a three-dimensional model. There, a flat or "birds-eye" version was rendered which simulates a direct overhead view of the region (the end sheets on both inside covers of this book were reproduced from this version). The flat version was then tilted in order to create a view of the area from an angle 23 degrees off the horizon. Shadows, textures, and colors were added to represent a view that one might see from space.

A two-thousand-foot pass isn't that hard a climb if a llama is carrying all your gear, and we enjoyed a leisurely lunch by the stone shelter house at Gunsight Pass, letting the stiff breeze cool us off as we absorbed both the view and the idea of being on the Continental Divide. From now on, all the water we saw would be draining to the Flathead Valley, the Columbia River, and the Pacific Ocean. Looking west down from the pass, we could see our next destination, Lake Ellen Wilson, about a thousand feet lower and a couple of miles hiking away. All the way down, the llamas, especially Zerc, scanned the goats on the nearby hillsides nervously, occasionally blasting another alarm into Marsha's ear to make sure we didn't spend too much time enjoying the long, flower-bordered cascades that tumbled from various snowfields and glacial remnants high on the slopes of Mount Jackson to our south. It worked; Marsha, surly and nearing deafness in one ear, insisted we keep moving until we were at the lake.

But that evening, the goats abandoned their highlands and joined us in camp. Habituated to people by several decades of foot traffic, the Gunsight goats spend nights right in the camping area, where they seek out the salt left where people and livestock have urinated or the sweet taste of toothpaste spit on the vegetation (they've even been known to lick sweat from the arms and legs of hikers, but we didn't get that cozy with them). This familiarity, both charming and dismaying, at least allowed me to get some close photographs, but when I looked at the pictures later, all seemed unreal. My mind kept insisting that goats that close must be stuffed.

These animals, which I've always admired as a great symbol of remote and untouchable wildness, brushed past our tent all night, clambering around on boulders and repeatedly approaching the llamas. I don't think Zerc slept at all; every hour or so he'd cut loose again, and I'd wake up wondering if the other llamas wished he'd shut up, too.

Repose

It rained during the night. Between that and Zerc's hourly goat reports, I probably didn't sleep much better than he did, but I was more or less asleep at about five when I was roused by distant thunder. At first I thought we were in for a bigger storm, but then I recognized it as an avalanche, somewhere out along the cirque. It occurred to me for about the thousandth time that nature keeps being nature all night long, even when we sack out and stop paying attention. Gravity never forgets.

Next morning, it was Jeremy who visually spotted the slide. The day before, we'd noticed a small glacial trough on the steep slopes along the south shore of the lake opposite our campsite—a place where a small glacier had carved a narrow path through the rock, with its terminal moraines down close to the lake shore. The long, slanting snow- and ice-field that covered the bottom of this trough may or may not have been what was left of the glacier. At the head of the trough perched a pile of big boulders and car-sized chunks of ice. During the

Weathered stone and wood on the shore of Lake Ellen Wilson suggest that everything exposed to the elements becomes rounder with time.

BEARS AND BERRIES

As an avid student of bears and their world, it may be that the first specific information I ever learned about Glacier had to do with its plants. In my first years as a ranger-naturalist in Yellowstone in the early 1970s, I often heard (and even repeated) the erroneous but popular common knowledge that Yellowstone was poor bear habitat when compared to a place like Glacier, because Glacier has lots of berries. About the only thing that turned out to be true about that unfortunate local wisdom was the part about the berries. When I was a child in Pennsylvania, my dad took me huckleberry picking in some great berry country, but even so, I'd never seen anything like the trails of Glacier. It isn't just that there are so many kinds—huckleberries, elderberries, raspberries, thimbleberries, kinnickinik, serviceberries, strawberries, bunchberries, and buffaloberries (to name only some of the ones you can eat, and ignoring the ones you shouldn't)—but that there are so many of them out there, to the delight of bears as well as human foragers.

The tall stalks of bear grass tower over patches of subalpine spiraea on the hillsides around Lake Ellen Wilson.

night, this stuff, many tons of it, finally surrendered to the heat of summer and broke free, crashing and sliding the length of the ice field (leaving a series of straight white scars on the gray old snow) and through the opening between the two terminal moraines, coming to rest in a scatter on the lowest slopes. It all seemed a little distant in the morning light, like a model-train layout, but remembering the power of its thunder, I realized it would have been a terrifying, exhilarating thing to witness standing on one of those moraines.

Predators at Last

We got an earlier start the next morning, having ten miles between us and the next cirque. Jeremy went ahead to shoo the goats away from the trail so Zerc wouldn't freak out again, then we moved steadily up, climbing a thousand feet in about a mile toward Lincoln Pass. As the lake receded below us, we came even with its abrupt west end, where its outlet stream drops more than thirteen hundred feet over a series of cascades and Beaver Chief Falls, most of which we couldn't see for the intervening ridge and trees. It's not as hard a climb as Gunsight Pass, but for some reason Lincoln Pass is the one that reminds me of novelist and Glacier Park enthusiast Mary Roberts Rinehart's definition of "pass," written in 1918: "A pass is a thing which you try to forget at the time, and which you boast about when you get back home."

We moved north and west down from the pass, occasionally catching glimpses of Lake McDonald off to the west, and stopped for some snacks and a chat with the keeper at Sperry Chalet (indefinitely closed for major refurbishing). We spent the early afternoon winding the five miles down Sprague Creek to Crystal Ford, then hiked noisily, very noisily, through the thick, high, and very limited visibility scrub up Snyder Creek toward our third cirque at Snyder Lake.

On the trail, when we weren't taking pictures of the scenery, the llamas, or Kessie (all equally irresistible subjects), we were usually wondering about bears, especially on trails like this one, which was famous both for berries and bears. We were just a little late for the peak of berry season, but friends had told us the "hucks" should still be good. By now, Kessie had developed a keen eye for berries, regularly instructing whichever parent carried her to stop at this or that bush—a huck here, a thimbleberry there. Her face was often smeared purple, and all that sugar and goo sluiced through her young system at an alarming rate. The most pressing supply-related question of the trip was whether or not the diapers would hold out.

But berries meant bears, especially here along Snyder Creek. I had every expectation of seeing some, or at least seeing what had sluiced through *their* systems. Even though I could have gotten some mileage out of a grizzly bear encounter for this chapter, I'm just as glad I didn't see them (every time Kessie called to one of us in that sweet, high-pitched little doll voice, I could imagine a bear or lion perking up its ears). What I saw instead was just as good, maybe better.

The folded strata of Gunsight Mountain, viewed from Gunsight Pass, give testimony to the past violence of a now-quiet landscape. Gunsight Lake is at the lower right, about 1,600 feet below the spot where this photograph was taken.

Snyder Lake rests in a rounded bowl of rock, the lower of two small ponds nestled right in a dense forest on the cirque floor. It feels a little cramped, with the walls of rock looming straight up from the forest around you, and in the evening, when we arrived, I found it pretty gloomy. But in the morning, it seemed a very exciting place, and I eagerly glassed the little pockets of meadow high on the slopes for signs of wildlife. Then, Marsha and I waited quietly in the morning chill at the little food preparation area not far from the campsites. We knew Kessie would roust her parents soon, and it was nice to be awake, hungry, and waiting.

We were rewarded when a tiny, dark weasel scooted out of the brush, climbed onto a log, and checked us out. I pulled my little camera from my pocket and ran off three or four hasty shots (they came out only good enough to prove I saw a weasel, showing its dark brown back and buff belly) before it ran back into the bushes. I see bears a lot more often than I see weasels, so my day was made almost before it began.

After a long, slow breakfast, at which we exchanged the sort of hygiene-related war stories that seem to come up toward the end of a long, bathless hike (Jeremy won with a tale of a month without a shower in the Himalayas), I took my little video camera for a walk to the far side of the pond, where a steep rock wall was crumbling into talus slopes right down to the water's edge. I wanted to get a look at the inlet stream, which emerged from a tight stone defile in the trees, but I never got that far. As I stopped to check the talus for pikas, whose little chirps of alarm I could hear, a larger, lighter weasel suddenly popped into view. I got about a half a minute of wobbly video of this one as it launched itself across the talus, bounding from rock to rock, stopping here and there to poke its head up, and finally disappearing. Only a mountain lion or a wolf would have been more exciting, but not by much. I couldn't wait to get back to the others and brag.

The Inland Coast

Last mornings on hikes are complicated. I can't keep from looking ahead to what I'll be doing when I'm out of the backcountry, but I regret that the trip is over (Jeremy observed that "By the time we finish this hike, we'll be in good enough shape to start it"). By now we were old hands at packing the llamas, who hummed softly as we did so. We never knew for sure if they were objecting, commiserating with one another, or even expressing enthusiasm that we were on our way again; it almost seemed they knew, perhaps by the relative lightness of the load, that we were almost home. Kessie fueled up at one final huckleberry bush, and we were on our way. It's only about four miles from Snyder Lake to the trailhead at Lake McDonald, and it's all downhill, so we were in for an easy hike.

The last couple of miles were among the most welcoming anyway, passing through the great cedar-hemlock forests that encircle the east end of Lake McDonald. We were suddenly strolling through what appeared to be a maritime forest, like those along the Pacific

Coast, five hundred miles to the west. With its high precipitation, humid local climate, and moderate temperatures and wind speeds, this is one of the most surprising and refreshing walking areas in the park, whether on the trail down from Snyder Lake or on the nearby Trail of the Cedars and the hike to Avalanche Lake.

At first when I'm in a forest like this, all I can do is gape at the grandness—the towering western hemlocks, whose trunks I always remember better than their soft, rubbery branches; the ragged-bark red cedars with their feathery branches, so like the junipers close to my home in Wyoming; and the western larch, with their ponderosa-pine-like bark, their splaying branch arrangement, and their habit of shedding their needles every fall. But the big trees aren't really what set the mood here. It's the heavy, often lush understory from which the big trunks emerge—not just the fern and maple and huckleberry and all the other shrubs, but the ground-hugging plants as well. In fact, it may actually be these smallest plants that most inspire the cathedral image so often invoked to express the mood of these forests. Certainly the light filtering through the high boughs and the architecturally uniform trunks bring to mind vaulted sanctuary ceilings and windows, but it's the 50 to 90 percent ground coverage of the mosses and the visual softening of the various hanging lichens and fungi that give these woods their reverential hush.

But soon we were out. We led the llamas down to the road, waited for a break in the traffic (jarring, noisy cars after so many miles of soft llama tread), and crossed to the lodge parking lot. Here we sorted our gear from the panniers and otherwise prepared for our respective long drives home. Larry showed up with his trailer right on time at two o'clock, listened calmly to our various adventures and revelations about goats, and accepted our thanks and a check. Then the llamas were loaded and out of our lives before we even realized how much we would miss them.

Almost immediately, for me at least, the country we'd just crossed, with its lingering glaciers, bragging-size passes, bright-eyed wildlife, and smoke-tinted light, became a little unreal. When I have to describe Glacier to someone who hasn't been there, my mind fills with the feelings of the country, and my mouth trips over inadequate adjectives. The magic of it never leaves me, but when I'm not there I'm haunted by the insufficiency of my memory to do it justice.

Late afternoon light
on Lake McDonald.

The Trail of the
Cedars is one of the
great ecological sur-
prises of Glacier
National Park, a little
bit of the Northwest
Coast transported far
inland.

I have a habit in Glacier National Park that I have nowhere else. I pick up little rocks, study them for a minute, then look up to the mountains to find their parents. This leads me to consider all manner of connections and processes.

If I happen to be high on a dry slope at the time, the rock will be sharp and jagged: a freshly fallen, randomly faceted, coarse-surfaced little thing whose shape I involuntarily attempt to recognize—an arrowhead, a cashew, a guitar pick, a badge. If it's flat (and most are flatter along one plane or another) I reflexively fit it into the curve between my thumb and forefinger, testing its heft and promise as a skipping-stone though I may be miles from open water.

If I happen to be loafing on the shore of a lake—let's say one of the long, deep ones that radiate out from the central mountain spines of the park—I find a whole different class of rocks. They have the same general assortment of shapes, usually flattened rather than round, and they come in the same colors, made much brighter by being wet. But their contours are softer; there are no sharp angles and edges, no fresh fractures, no raspy friction against the thumb. Again I look up to the mountains to see if I can figure out where each piece started.

I'm rarely sure I can tell. The sheer mountain faces two or three thousand feet above me are splotchy, weathered, lichen-coated, and often

Iceberg Lake, at the end of a side spur off the Ptarmigan Tunnel Trail, sports an annual flotilla of small icebergs from the permanent snowfield along the lake's shore.

A REALM OF PASSES

THRUSTS, FAULTS, AND OTHER GEOLOGICAL ACROBATICS

deceptively lighted; none of them bear a lot of resemblance to the smooth, wetly shining little rock I hold in my hand. But I keep trying, and I suspect I make the right guess fairly often. That dark horizontal band there, about two-thirds of the way up, that the geology guidebooks would call green but which looks to me like a kind of muddy slate—that's probably where this little rock came from.

Geology is a pretty hard sell for most people because it demands so many leaps of faith. The geologist tells a story of biblical proportions, an epic tale of continent-sized plates of earth crust ponderously slamming around the planet, grinding into each other at speeds that makes glaciers seem like cheetahs, and setting off all kinds of titanic "lesser actions" on their surface: mountain building, volcanism, seas ebbing and flowing, and all the other stuff that we always thought was a pretty big deal. It's hard to think of the Rocky Mountains, or even some individual mountain, as being merely a side effect of some *really* big event. By the time geologists get down to explaining what happened in a specific place, such as Glacier, we're so overwhelmed by the cosmic magnitude of the big picture that we can't take in the local neighborhood.

But I'm interested, and so I follow the geologists and their guidebooks as they interpret various spots on the landscape and create a biography of the past billion or so years, confident that their explanations will be obvious to anyone with the sense God gave a goose. I trust them, but I reserve some doubt, and feel a little foolish asking them where this little rock came from.

No matter how often I read or hear the geological story, simple little questions linger in my mind. How come this rock in my hand is green in the first place? How long does it take a rock to get from the top to the bottom? Do the rocks usually start out as big ones and break up on the way down? Do the ones breaking off today stand a chance of reaching the lake, now that there are so many other rocks piled up in the way? How much of the smoothing is done while the rock is on its way down, and how much is done after it comes to rest in the lake and is sloshed around with other rocks by a few thousand years of waves? And what happens next? Will all these rocks go somewhere else later?

The Long Story

I don't blame the geologists for my bewilderment about geology, of course, any more than I blame General Motors because I don't really understand automatic transmissions. And historically, my geological bewilderment puts me in very good company here in Glacier. For more than a century, a string of distinguished explorers and geologists has been poking around here, gradually answering the really important questions, then reconsidering them, then answering them again.

Helena formation rocks may be gray upon first exposure but typically weather to a lighter shade of tan.

Left: Travelers on the Going-to-the-Sun Road in eastern Glacier National Park have only a few chances to see the Altyn formation, along the shore of St. Mary Lake.

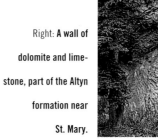

Right: A wall of dolomite and lime-stone, part of the Altyn formation near St. Mary.

Right: The more distinctive layering of the Grinnell formation suggests variations in ocean depth during the time of deposition.

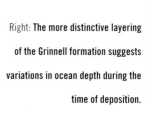

Left: Lichens add brightness to this slab of the Appekun[?] formation, one of th[e] park's most diverse colorful rock.

so that billion-and-a-half-year-old rock rests solidly on rock not a tenth as old. Another exception, itself only less spec-tacular by comparison to the stupendous fact of the over-thrust, is the "sill," where a layer of molten rock was forced between layers of the sedimen-tary rock, resulting in dark bands and veins. These sills often have a lighter "halo" above and below them, where their heat altered and faded the sedimentary rock, thus highlighting the sill even fur-ther from the surrounding layers.

We are accustomed to thinking only of the surface of the land because that is all we can see and admire. But while beauty is only skin deep, geology goes clear through. It is a useful

mental exercise (greatly facilitated by a good topographic or geologic map) to stand in front of a certain formation and try to track it through the mountain range: imagine where it reappears on the other side, and watch for it when you are

Most of Clements Mountain is com-posed of Snowslip formation rock, but the highest part of the peak is a remnant of the Shepard formation.

Right: McDonald Creek exposes and brightens some of the park's most colorful rock—in this case, the potholed Prichard formation.

Redrock Falls, on Swiftcurrent Creek, flows over reddish Grinnell argillite.

Right: A closer view of the layers of the Grinnell formation.

Left: Contrasting shades of Grinnell formation rock along the Gunsight Pass Trail.

STROMATOLITES

various places in the park. To the casual observer, they are evident as circular patterns and disruptions in the otherwise relatively straight strata. Some of the most pronounced are likened to cabbages, and may be revealed as twisting bulges and columns of rock several feet across. Where prehistoric conditions

Most of the rock in Glacier was put there before life got very complicated; these huge cliffs contain no dinosaurs or even fish ancestors to speak of. They do, however, contain countless fossils of algae, known as stromatolites, which lived in the shallower portions of the seas and are now visible at

(presumably such things as nutrient availability, water temperature, and sunlight) were right, stromatolites thrived, and their fossils now exist in beds as much as one hundred feet thick.

SEDIMENTS AND SILLS

Compared to many landscapes, whose original rock strata are twisted and rolled almost beyond understanding, the geological biography of Glacier & Waterton is simple, with one spectacular exception. The simple part is the "layer cake" of sedimentary rock that is visible on the sheer faces of the glacially carved peaks all over the park. Though a first glance is often not sufficient to distinguish exactly which of the layers you're seeing, they are almost always neatly displayed, each horizontally atop the other, each younger than the one below it, altogether portraying the final third of the earth's 4.5-billion-year story.

As these layers accumulated, their mass pressed down on the older, lower layers, altering them structurally to form the argillites, siltites, and other rocks visible today. But in many places it is still obvious even to the amateur observer that these rocks are the product of sedimentation—the imponderably time-consuming process by which fine particles of mineral, shell, bone, and other matter slowly settle out of the water and gradually deepen on the ocean floor. Here and there, in a surprising number of places, flat rocks still show the ripples of wave-washed sand, and in a few other places, the patterns of simple fossil algae, stromatolites, are exposed.

The spectacular exception to this neat story is the Lewis Overthrust, visible in some places along the east and south edges of the park. Here, the ancient sedimentary layers have slid over much younger rocks,

Standing alone and straddling the park boundary south of St. Mary, 8,665-foot. Divide Mountain is composed mostly of Proterozoic rocks of the Altyn formation, the oldest rocks visible on the eastern side of Glacier Park.

Below, right, and lower right:
Cameron Falls, near Waterton
Townsite, washes over Waterton
formation rocks, among the oldest in
either Waterton or Glacier.

Ripples formed on an ancient beach
now reside near Gunsight Pass, with
the deformed Empire and Helena
formation strata of Gunsight
Mountain in the background.

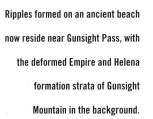

next over there. Eventually this sort of thinking will help connect you to the landscape in a way very different from learning about its watersheds or plant communities.

Everything that has happened to this landscape since the sediments were deposited—glaciers carving troughs and cirques, rivers building up loamy valleys, rock-, mud-, and snow-slides ripping material from the steep slopes and piling it up below, plants and animals slowly littering and enriching the soil—can complicate and obscure the local picture. But if you stand back far enough, the big picture, of sediments and sills, can still be clearly seen.

M E T A P H O R I C A L   M O U N T A I N S

Glacier's scenery has exhausted the adjectival resources of many writers. Some retreated into breathlessness, others strained toward some unachievable metaphorical power, others collapsed into statistical security, incanting elevations and distances as if numbers could bring it all to life. But some writers, both technical and popular, have come pretty close to capturing the feel if not the scale of the place,

they were reminding me of something, but I just couldn't call it to mind. Then one day recently I was looking at some slides taken on a backcountry trip. There was one of me standing in the rain with a high, vaguely pyramidal peak behind me, and suddenly I had it. Though they never looked much like the pyramids of Egypt to me, I was suddenly struck by their similarity to certain Mayan pyramids, ones I'd seen more than twenty years earlier at Tikal in

usually when they compared what they saw with something more familiar. The sheared-off faces of the mountains do in fact bring to mind the prows of ships, though those ships would be the size of asteroids. The cirques—those lovely, high, little mountain-backed coves—have repeatedly been compared with the work of someone with a giant ice-cream scoop, and some are perfect enough to have been left by such a device.

On the other hand, I have yet to see a mountain, here or anywhere else, that looked even faintly like a throne. Throne imagery has been popular here, but it only works, I suspect, because it invokes royalty, and there is something imperially grand about this landscape.

It took me many years to sort out the faint sense of recognition these mountains gave me. I was occasionally aware that

Guatemala. With their stepped and often very steep sides, their intricate facades, and their perpendicular caps, the Mayan temples seem to me perfect stylized versions of glaciated peaks. A few centuries of weathering, crumbling, and general collapse since the end of the Mayan era have only made the similarities more pronounced.

As it happens, most of Glacier's geological history is fairly sedate. Practically all of the rock you see, whether attached to a mountain or easing its way down toward a valley bottom, was laid down as sediment at the bottom of various inland seas, layer upon layer and thousands of feet thick. This process started about a billion and a half years ago.

I never use numbers like these without mentally making sweeping gestures to indicate their staggering imprecision: a billion here, a billion there, as the saying goes. Glacier's oldest rocks are from 1.6 billion to 800 million years old and were all laid down during the sprawling Proterozoic Eon. After the Proterozoic, sediments continued to build up for another 300 or so million years, through the Paleozoic Era, but in Glacier none of the Paleozoic sediments remain. They all have been eroded away during the past 200 million years, leaving only the much older rocks.

Another troubling thing about geologists is the ease with which they identify these ancient layers, mainly by the specific colors they see. They confidently describe rocks or whole strata as red, or yellow, or green, or any other obvious color, even though the real hues are often more subtle than that. Even the ones that are only one color are rarely a simple color. The ones that are called red may actually be a nice, honest red, but most are more like a faded-brick red, or maybe a vegetable-soup red, or a mahogany brown, or some other equivocal shade. The yellows are often more like dusty tans, or old-chewing-gum-under-a-chair gray, than a real yellow. And the greens range from mint licorice to grasshopper green. Subtleties abound. But if you line the bottom of a shallow stream with a mixture of these rocks on a sunny day, you have a show superior to anything in Tiffany's window.

Two main factors influenced the original rocks' colors: the amount of iron minerals involved in their creation and the depth of the water in which they were deposited. If they contained sufficient iron (usually in the form of hematite, but sometimes pyrite), and the water was shallow enough for oxygen to be available, the resulting color would be some variation on rust: reddish, brownish, maroonish, even purplish. Greens and grays usually result from an oxygen-deprived environment (that is, formation occurred in deeper water, say a hundred feet or more), where heat and pressure altered the chemical character of the rock, turning it into chlorite.

So far, this summary is tidy, though incomplete. As the ocean floor rose and fell, alternating bands of reddish and greenish rocks were created in the bed. With enough heat and pressure, both types became darker minerals—magnetite or biotite. The rocks least influenced by these various chemical processes were likely to be simple tans. To add to the difficulty of figuring out what the colors mean, all the rocks have been subjected to weathering, fading, and all kinds of other influences, including lichens and mosses that obscure their colors.

Besides, the creation of these layers of rock resulted from more than just the simple deposition of sediment. Occasional subterranean movements of molten earth, under

fabulous temperatures and pressures, forced "sills," or layers of other material in between existing layers in the stack. Not only did these sills add yet another color (usually a very dark one) into the mix, but their intense heat also bleached out the sedimentary rocks above and below them, creating a pale "halo" around the sill.

Here is a brief tour of the layers of sediment in Glacier and Waterton, starting with the oldest, which are on the bottom. The oldest visible formation in the two parks is the Waterton, which appears only on the Canadian side of the border. If you're hoping to identify formations by their colors, the Waterton shows how difficult this is. One geologist, in describing the Waterton, said, "Although a fresh surface is red-brown or gray, the dolomite weathers to gray, tan, or reddish brown." That's quite a range of color, and it's only one formation.

The oldest visible rock—a billion or so years in age—on the American side is the Altyn formation, as much as twenty-three hundred feet thick and usually tan. It can only be seen on the east side of the park. Altyn was the name of either an early miner or another miner's horse. It may have been the name of both—and who knows for which the formation is named? The first three thousand feet above the Altyn formation is occupied by the Appekunny formation, apparently named for James Willard Schultz, who lived much of his long life in the region and celebrated its wild country and native inhabitants in many books. The Blackfeet gave him this name (the preferred spelling for most purposes is Apikuni), which means "spotted robe." The formation is dominated by greenish and grayish shalelike rocks, known as argillites and siltites. Above it is the thinner (about eight hundred feet) and mostly gray Empire formation. The Grinnell formation, named for the great naturalist and conservationist George Bird Grinnell (Schultz's friend), is layered above it as thick as fourteen hundred feet and is most known for some of the brightest, most obvious reds in the park. Grinnell is often credited with fathering Glacier National Park, and this seems like the sort of monument he would have appreciated.

Above the Grinnell is the Helena formation, twenty-five hundred feet of grays and tans, the Prichard formation, four thousand feet of dark grays and near-blacks, the Snowslip formation, fourteen hundred feet of numerous pale shades, and the Shepard formation, six hundred feet of grays, greens, and yellows that cap some of the most prominent peaks in the center of the park. Of all the formations, the Helena is the one with the most pronounced sills—haloed, dark-gray bands toward the top of some of the most spectacular peaks.

Now if you were adding while you read the previous three paragraphs, you noticed that these layers add up to 15,000 feet of sediment. You may also know that the highest point in Glacier is 10,466-foot Mount Cleveland, which rises only about 7,300 feet above Lake McDonald. So, you may wonder, how can there be 15,000 feet of sediments in 7,300 feet of elevation change? Good question.

V isitors to Glacier/Waterton may be struck by the raw, almost lifeless character of the landscape, such as this view of Snowmelt Pond near Sexton Glacier. The parks are such good geological classrooms because their lessons are so clearly exposed.

Thrusts and Faults

About 65 million years ago ("give or take 10 million," as geologist Gary Alt has written), this landscape began to take on features recognizable in the modern park topography. The big event was the Lewis Overthrust, in which an enormous slab of these sediments, all the way down to the Altyn formation, separated from its neighbors and from its foundation and began to move east. These masses are almost as incomprehensible as the time spans involved, but it went roughly like this.

Picture two boards, several feet long and a foot wide, lying north to south. One lies directly on top of the other, and they are held together by a nail at the south end. The top board is the overthrust slab, whose northern end will move the greatest distance. Now push the top board toward the east; it will "hinge" at the nail. In the case of the Lewis Overthrust, the hinge is more than sixty miles south of the park, near the west fork of the Sun River.

As the top slab moved east, away from the adjoining land to the west, a gap was created, quite a big one, and we now call this the valley of the North Fork Flathead River, which runs along the west side of the park. West of this ten-mile-wide valley, the Whitefish Mountain Range is composed of the same rocks, in the same layers, as those in the park to the east. And the slab moved on.

If you drive west toward Glacier National Park from Browning, Montana—from the lower country known as the Great Plains—you see ahead of you the Rocky Mountain Front, a wall of towering peaks and ridges. The perhaps overly lyrical writers who describe mountains as seeming to march forward in ranks would not be far wrong here; you are looking at what's left of the leading edge—the "front"—of the overthrust slab, which marched this far and came to rest on younger rock.

Geologists have now mapped the "fault," or the front edge, of this overthrust for more than 250 miles, from far south of the "hinge" to well into Canada. In some places, the total eastward movement of the slab was probably as much as fifty miles. The thickness of the material in the slab ranges from a few hundred feet near the hinge to more than six thousand feet up in the park.

The overthrust presented early scientific explorers with a pretty puzzle. When Bailey Willis and his colleagues came here in 1901, their most startling discovery must have been made along this front, where they found relatively young Cretaceous rocks, not much more than 100 million years old, resting directly underneath the billion-year-old Altyn formation, which itself sat at the bottom of a pile of other formations that were all much older than the Cretaceous. In 1902, Bailey formally recognized the nature of what had happened and named this mass the Lewis Overthrust.

But for all the motion of the overthrust, the land still bore only faint resemblance to its modern appearance. For the next 60 million years or so it continued to change

The red Grinnell argillite of Red Rock Canyon, in northern Waterton Lakes National Park, almost glows under its film of moisture.

FOLLOWING PAGES:

The Lewis Overthrust is exposed at Sofa Mountain, near the Chief Mountain International Highway in southeastern Waterton Lakes National Park. Here, the higher slopes of the mountain are composed of ancient (at least a billion-year-old) rocks resting upon much younger (100-million-year-old) Cretaceous rocks.

slowly. Streams carved steep canyons and tight little valleys into the sedimentary rocks, washing eroded material away to lower lands east and west. This process set the stage for the ice-sculpting that gave us the present park area, but before getting to that, I should return to the earlier question: How can fifteen thousand feet of sediment be identified in a seven-thousand-foot high mountain range? Some parts of the answer are subtle: the formations are not always at their maximum thickness, and some of the higher ones are completely or largely gone, eroded away.

But the most important part of the answer is that the formations are not flat. They lie in a syncline, a huge concavity running north and south up the middle of the park. Seen in an east-to-west cross-section, the formations visible in Glacier are not a straight layer cake; they sag—a lot—in the middle, as if the cake had been supported only on its east and west edges and the middle had drooped like a swayback horse. Thus, where they are exposed on the surface, the formations tend to slant inward, allowing a two-thousand-foot-thick layer, let's say, to gain only a few hundred feet in actual elevation.

Ice

Two or three million years ago, the earth cooled enough for enormous sheets of ice to form over much of the northern and southern ends of the globe. There were a series of these events, or ice ages, the last one ending about eleven thousand years ago.

A glacier is snow, fallen to great depths, packed to great mass, and brought to life by its own weight. More weight, more time, and more freezing-thawing cycles turn the snow to ice, which piles up until finally, at a depth of 150 to 200 feet, the whole thing begins to flow.

Flow is an important word here; the glacier doesn't just get heavy and slide down the hill. It takes on a kind of elasticity or flexibility, like liquid. It flows faster in the thick middle than on the thin edges, and on the top side than on the bottom, which must contend with the snagging friction of the valley floor. It also flows faster at the head (the upper end), where the most new snow and weight is being added, and at the snout (the front, or lower end), where it is most subject to melting in the warmer lower temperatures, than it does in the middle. It is hard to avoid thinking of a glacier as nearly a living thing.

During the last ice age, glaciers worked their way down into the valleys, joining others to form mighty ice streams that eventually flowed out onto the open plains as wide-lobed piedmont glaciers. Working from the existing network of drainages, they defined and reworked the major valleys of the present park. Ten miles long and a thousand feet thick, they flowed west out of the park area, where they joined other glaciers coming south from British Columbia, and east from the Whitefish Range, to fill the North Fork valley with a giant glacier half a mile thick. Farther south, more glaciers flowed from the west side of the Lewis Range,

Iceberg Lake with
Crowfoot Mountain
(left) and Mount Henkel
(right) in the distance.

joining in the valley of the Middle Fork Flathead River along the present park boundary. Parts of this ice flow actually backed up over Marias Pass, thus crossing the Continental Divide and joining the Two Medicine Glacier, which emerged onto the plains along the southeast edge of the present park. Up along the east side of the front, glaciers spread out onto the prairie from the smaller valleys, while the valleys along the northeastern side of the park filled with north-flowing glaciers that moved up into Canada from the St. Mary River valley, the Belly River valley, and others.

The retreat of these glaciers was dramatic and, by geological standards, almost sensationally abrupt. Twenty thousand years ago, the spread of ice was at its greatest. Nine thousand years later, 90 percent of that incredible ocean of ice was gone, and only a few high-elevation glaciers remained. But they left a magnificent legacy.

What the glaciers left was an improbably steep land, where all motion seems up and down, a constantly sidehilling, ridge-running kind of place. With my hiker's urge to see what's beyond these ridges, I see Glacier as a realm of passes, slightly less high places that allow me to move from one wonderland to the next.

What the glaciers left were two large mountain ranges. The Livingston Range runs down the western half of the park, from the Canadian border to Lake McDonald, while the Lewis Range runs the length of the park on the eastern side, from Canada to the gap we call Marias Pass. The streams flowing from these high ranges pool up in the narrow adjoining lowlands, creating on both sides of the park a series of long, roughly parallel lakes that give daily demonstrations of the pathetic inadequacy of the word "blue."

What the glaciers left was an intricate network of valleys, the comfortably rounded drainages characteristic of ice-carving. The valleys usually head in one or more cirques, and sometimes one mountain will have three or even four cirques, turning its remaining peak, or "horn" (recall the Matterhorn), into a narrow, squared-off spire or pyramid. When two glaciers chew away the rock between them, leaving only a thin wall, it is called an arête; the best-known one in the park is the Garden Wall, most easily visible from the Going-to-the-Sun Road. Where the arête has been broken through and worn into a gentle saddle, it is called a col. Many if not most of the passes around the park are cols.

Where a small, high glacier once flowed into a much larger and lower glacier, the retreating ice often left a high valley that ends abruptly in a cliff; such a valley is called a hanging valley, and the park is full of these, too—intimate little paradises that often hide two or three small lakes and all sorts of other wonders, and they drain in one or two long waterfalls that plunge down to the larger valley below.

What the glaciers left was one of the most tortuous, abrupt, and neck-straining drainage systems in North America. All those horns and cols and hanging valleys, with all their remaining snowfields and ice, shed the glacial melt and snowmelt and summer rain in

T*his view over Grinnell Glacier and Upper Grinnell Lake from the top of the Garden Wall, near the Highline Trail, exposes the sweep and flow of a still-active glacier.*

long, waving threads of water that always surprise you as you approach them, their roar awakening you to their true size and volume. High-gradient streams, maybe beyond counting and certainly beyond naming, rush across the angled slabs of red and green and gray; they finally come to rest in lakes and ponds, from the smallest secret tarns resting in the most remote cirques to the long, landmark lakes that support a vast postcard industry.

What the glaciers left, however, was very little in the way of glaciers. Those that remain continue to shrink and vanish, from 150 in the mid-1800s to about 50 very small ones now. The largest, Blackfoot Glacier, occupies little more than 400 acres. The two most often cited, Sperry (reduced from 960 acres in the mid-1800s to 250 acres today) and Grinnell (from 585 to 225), reflect a worldwide trend of global climate warming that humans are probably now accelerating.

So maybe the most important legacy the glaciers left is a landscape still wild and unaltered enough to tell us about ourselves and the way we treat the planet. This park is the sort of place that leads to such reflections. As I stand on a high col between cirques, ducking behind a low screen of trees as a sleet storm passes over, I alternately wonder about very little questions and very big ones.

I wonder if humans can last long enough for our effects on the climate to eventually show up in the same kind of phenomenally ancient stone biography I see reaching up the mountainside before me.

And as I absently toe the rock rubble at my feet, I wonder if all these little sharp-edged rocks, so fresh from their respective formations, will have to wait for the next glacier to come by before they can get down to the bottom.

And I'm not sure which is the big question and which is the little.

T he ice high on the facing ridge over Upper Grinnell Lake rests in the same plane as the park's most prominent igneous sill, whose darker rock is "haloed" by heat-altered sedimentary rock.

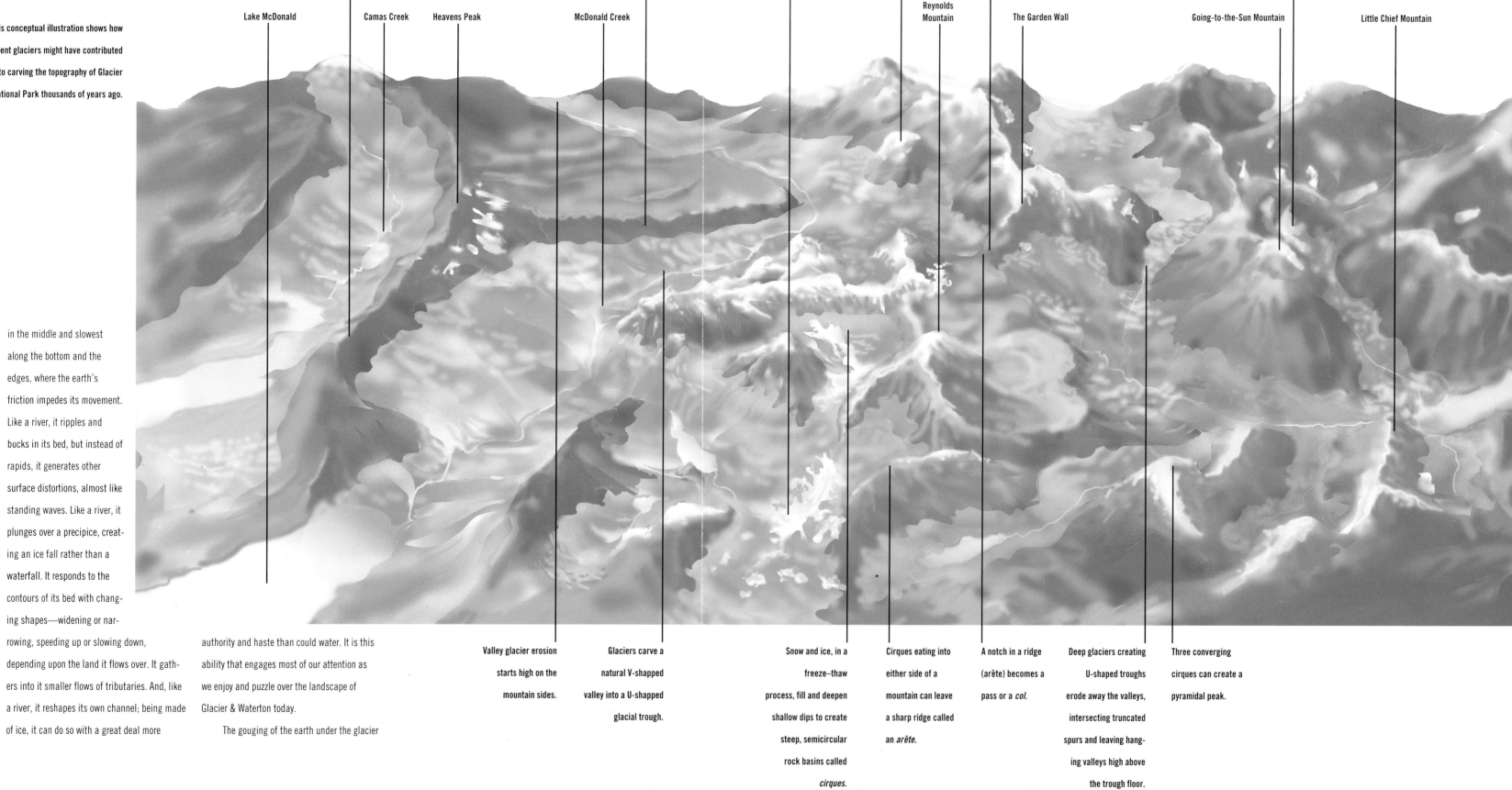

This conceptual illustration shows how ancient glaciers might have contributed to carving the topography of Glacier National Park thousands of years ago.

Lake McDonald

Stanton Mountain

Camas Creek

Heavens Peak

McDonald Creek

Glacier Wall

Sperry Glacier

Haystack Butte

Reynolds Mountain

Logan Pass

The Garden Wall

Going-to-the-Sun Mountain

Sexton Glacier

Little Chief Mountain

Goat Mountain

in the middle and slowest along the bottom and the edges, where the earth's friction impedes its movement. Like a river, it ripples and bucks in its bed, but instead of rapids, it generates other surface distortions, almost like standing waves. Like a river, it plunges over a precipice, creating an ice fall rather than a waterfall. It responds to the contours of its bed with changing shapes—widening or narrowing, speeding up or slowing down, depending upon the land it flows over. It gathers into it smaller flows of tributaries. And, like a river, it reshapes its own channel; being made of ice, it can do so with a great deal more

authority and haste than could water. It is this ability that engages most of our attention as we enjoy and puzzle over the landscape of Glacier & Waterton today.

The gouging of the earth under the glacier

Valley glacier erosion starts high on the mountain sides.

Glaciers carve a natural V-shapped valley into a U-shapped glacial trough.

Snow and ice, in a freeze–thaw process, fill and deepen shallow dips to create steep, semicircular rock basins called cirques.

Cirques eating into either side of a mountain can leave a sharp ridge called an arête.

A notch in a ridge (arête) becomes a pass or a col.

Deep glaciers creating U-shaped troughs erode away the valleys, intersecting truncated spurs and leaving hanging valleys high above the trough floor.

Three converging cirques can create a pyramidal peak.

ANCIENT GLACIERS

I t may not be entirely accurate to think of the small glaciers that now linger in Glacier National Park as remnants of the last great ice age. It might be more correct to describe them as latter-day examples of the ice sheets that used to be everywhere in this region. The last ice age ended about 10,000 years ago and left only small, scattered glaciers here, which became smaller and smaller in the ensuing centuries and were almost or entirely gone just 500 years ago. Then the world entered a cooling period known as the Little Ice Age, which lasted until the mid-1800s and encouraged the reappearance of small glaciers. Since then, the park's fifty or so active glaciers have been shrinking again, and some are now only a quarter of the size they were in 1850. On a smaller scale, however, these modern glaciers are doing the same kinds of work done by their huge ancestors long ago.

It is admittedly difficult to stand beside or even above a glacier in today's park and immediately picture how it works. Typically, it occupies only a fraction of a huge cirque or valley carved by some immense, earlier

glacier and seems incapable of making much difference in the landscape. During a brief stay it will do nothing visible; it will just sprawl there on the slope, perhaps dripping a little water out below. But it is working all the time, whether growing or receding. The best analogy I have heard to explain the process compares the glacier to a river; after all, it's just very cold water, moving very slowly.

Like a river, the glacier does not flow at a uniform speed; it moves fastest

*S*exton Glacier and
waterfall.

Wild Goose Island **Red Eagle Lake**   **St. Mary Lake**

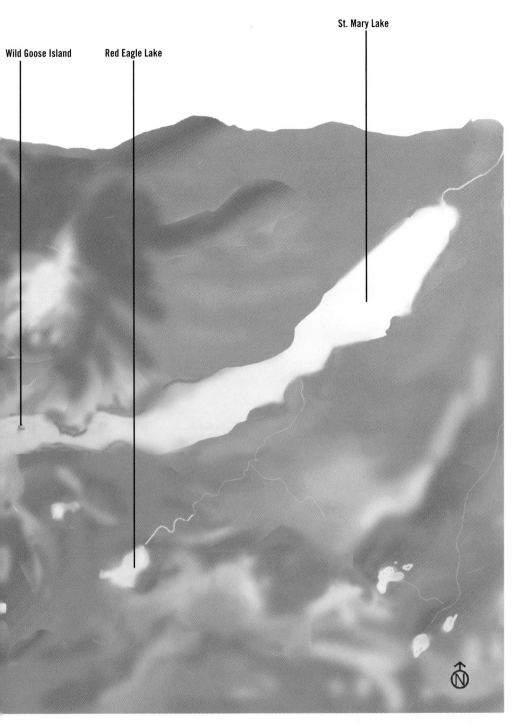

is perhaps the easiest part of this process to visualize. Next easiest may be the mounding of stone and earth beside the glacier's path (in lateral moraines) and in front of it (in terminal moraines). Again, like a river but more forcefully, the glacier adds rocks to its flow and lets them do most of the work of scouring and abrading the rocks they are continually pushed against. Less easy to picture are other processes, especially the one that allows the glacier to carve rock through a thawing-and-freezing action by repeatedly attaching ice to rock at its head, then plucking that rock loose.

When these processes are carried out across an entire mountain range by small cirque glaciers that drop into large valley glaciers, the eventual disappearance of the ice leaves a fantasy landscape of thin mountain walls, Matterhorn-style peaks, hanging valleys of Shangri-la beauty, and long, lacy waterfalls.

The mixture of sleet and snow blows over, but I'm too cold standing still and ruminating on the fate of small, if ancient, stones. I'm only good for a little while with the big questions—then I need to concentrate on simpler things, like how to extract junk food from my pack without having to stop and take it off (we all need quixotic quests like this). My biologist friend and I take a last look down into the cirque we've just climbed from and prepare to head down the trail.

But it's impossible to stop looking out far away from where I stand. This landscape is always grabbing you and spinning you around, demanding that you absorb yet another fantasy vista and consider yet another beckoning pass astride some distant ridge.

From our current pass, at about seven thousand feet, peaks rise abruptly on both sides, all raw rock, lingering ice, and a little fresh snow and sleet from earlier today. Scanning the high mountains and walls to the east, where we are heading next, I think I can discern a cirquelike character to things, but I could be looking into parts of two or three different ones. I'm sure that the country below has been shaped by glaciers, but there are no textbook-neat, rounded-out alcoves presenting themselves from this view-point. It's all more ragged than that,

EMERALD MOUNTAINS
TENACITY AND SURRENDER IN THE FOREST

with distant ribbons of icemelt undulating off vertical faces, and the whole convoluted bowl before me drops off out of sight at an angle to the northeast. At my feet, grayish snowbanks, dwindling with almost visible reluctance in the equivocal late-spring weather, wind in long narrow curves along the ridge and up into sheltered pockets at the base of the cliffs. There's life up there, but not much.

Zone Walking

For many years, biologists and ecologists have divided dramatic landscapes like this into life zones, broad horizontal bands of organic communities draped over the inorganic layers of earth and stone. And if the geological layers seem jumbled and puzzling, the organic ones approach the chaotic, getting less easy to visually define and mentally pigeonhole the farther downhill you get. Biologist Vernon Bailey, in *Wild Animals of Glacier National Park* (1918), one of the park's classics (still engaging today for all its dated material), admitted right off that "only by a broad view can the zonal arrangement be recognized." As near as I have been able to tell, the broad view is usually the one you get from several miles off, like from this pass.

The highest zone, starting just above me, is the most visually commanding and least hospitable: the walls, cliffs, horns, and other sheer rock forms of the mountaintops. From any distance, the cliffs look bare, with no potential for plant life. But a variety of mosses and lichens do just fine up there. In the countless little niches and cavities and crevices that pock the sedimentary layers, other plants get by, too: a sparse tuft of grass here, a stunted shrub or subalpine fir only a few inches high there.

At the pass we're standing more or less at the treeline, the upper limit of marginal hospitality for such large and needy plants. At Glacier, treeline varies by more than a thousand feet, depending upon local conditions, including steepness and substance of the slope, wind, and aspect (which direction the slope faces, north being the harshest climate but also the wettest).

Up here, where the inorganic landscape is at its most baldly monumental, everything alive is in miniature. There are temporarily luxurious mats of "cushion growth," where a variety of ground-hugging herbaceous plants cover whatever soil they can find. Some of the most sensational, if subtle, flower shows occur here among the many "bellyflowers" (so named because you have to get on yours to enjoy them). One of my slides from this hike shows a big muddy hiking boot (apparently in the picture for scale, but maybe just by mistake) along the edge of a grand patch of moss campion, whose tiny blossoms were once known as mountain pinks.

A few hundred yards down the trail from the pass, we cross a sloping meadow thick with glacier lilies, whose little bulbs are a favored bear food (as if I needed yet another reminder to keep a watch for bears). The trees at these elevations—usually some mixture of

Northern American forests are underappreciated for their diversity of life. These brilliantly colored lichens are only a few of the 425 species of that simple life form that inhabit Glacier National Park.

The western hemlock–western red cedar forest along Avalanche Creek on Glacier's west side brings a bit of the Pacific Northwest to the park and a cathedral-like hush to the Trail of the Cedars.

subalpine fir, whitebark pine, and Engelmann spruce—make a living by conceding every possible authority to their environment. Most of all, they survive by remaining small and short.

Perhaps because they are so reminiscent of tiny forests in childhood fairy tales, or perhaps because their small size makes them so easy to enjoy as somehow "complete" scenes, these little woods never fail to charm me. The first stream crossing, over a willow-bordered little stairstep of pools, has a Japanese-garden perfection. It's a Bonsai landscape of extraordinary beauty, and I am instantly struck with the peculiar desperation that comes from realizing the inadequacy of photographs. All I can do is look and surrender to its wonder, and go on.

Bailey's broad view can sometimes be surprisingly local. At this latitude, north-facing slopes are cooler than south-facing ones, so the north slopes hold moisture longer. Also, thanks to the generally west winds of this region, snow tends to pile up more on the north slopes as well, giving them even more of a moisture advantage. One effect of this is that the warmer, drier south slopes tend to have higher timberlines. This means certain peaks can have one or more life zones at the same elevation, depending on aspect.

We drop quickly down the switchbacks into heavier and heavier vegetation. At about sixty-four hundred feet we pass a small, unnamed pond; looking up from here, even my nongeologist's eye can discern several distorted cirques from which ice had once descended to round off all the contours around and below us. Some more switchbacks down the face of small cliffs, and we're well below six thousand feet and clearly into the next stage of Bailey's "zonal arrangement," the coniferous forests that cover about two-thirds of the park.

Here on the east side of Glacier, the most common trees are lodgepole pine, Engelmann spruce, Douglas fir, and subalpine fir, with pockets (some large) of aspen, cottonwood, and other deciduous trees. On the west side, for reasons I'll get to presently, there are more and different kinds of trees—western hemlock, western red cedar, western larch, paper birch, and a batch of others in addition to those most common on the east side.

In one open area, I pause long enough to take my thousandth poorly composed photograph of Indian paintbrush, probably my favorite flower, though here given stiff competition by yellow columbines, yellow violets, fleabane, and one of the billion or so daisylike flowers that, much like the varieties of sparrows, all look different to me but not in any memorable way. As always, however, the paintbrush gets most of my attention. Ever since my first visit to Glacier more than twenty years ago, I've been entertained by its seemingly endless number of shades—rose, salmon, fuschia, amber, candy apple red, arterial scarlet, baby-girl pink, canary yellow, lavender-gray—and on and on through all the countless variations of red and pink and yellow. To me, Indian paintbrush is the botanical equivalent of all those delicately shaded stones shining from shallow streambeds.

Continuing down the slope, we're soon into brush and undergrowth that is both higher and denser than the stunted krummholz ("crooked wood") forest higher up. I'm

Common bear grass dots a hillside near Old Man Lake. The pale cone is composed of hundreds of tiny blossoms that, though not of special interest to bears, are eaten by bighorn sheep and elk.

*S*mall ponds and wetlands in the park provide an important habitat for a variety of animals, from insects to waterfowl and moose.

*L*odgepole pine, so named for its use by Native Americans in the construction of shelters, is the most abundant pine in Glacier National Park. It is most common on the west side, in the valley of the North Fork of the Flathead River.

unaccustomed to so much lushness under the tree canopy, and to combat my unease I joke about the "cow-parsnip forest" as we walk past enormous versions of this plant that are taller than I am, mixed with devil's club, thimbleberry, alder, and false hellebore. Here and there, even in fairly heavy forest, bear grass towers over much of the undergrowth, its many tiny flowers forming a large white rounded cone as much as ten or twelve inches long. Many of these cones are not straight, but bend to one side and then swoop up, giving an impression, when seen in a group, of a floral ballet caught in mid-dip.

As we drop to five thousand feet and skirt a couple of larger lakes, we wind up as close to the "bottom" as you can get on this side of Glacier, following a river through a series of long meadows. After two days of rain (each time a new wave of the storm would hit us, one of us would mutter, "It's just a squall . . ."), the sun finally emerges, and the now-receding peaks look more inviting than they did when we were among them. We're nearly to the car, but if we continued on east, before long we would be out on the prairies of the Blackfeet Indian Reservation. At several points along the east side of the park, a "transition zone" of upland prairie crosses into the park, adding its birches, aspens, willows, and various prairie grasses and wildflowers to the park's cross-section of life communities. At the prairie's edge, you cross that other timberline, the lower limit of the forests.

The quickness with which one moves from one of these communities to another in the park is what has always distinguished Glacier in the eyes of naturalists. We passed through them all in just a few miles, but once you're out on the prairie, it's about a thousand miles or so east to the next zone.

East Side, West Side

I suspect that many casual observers, driving across the middle of the park—say from east to west—don't really notice any change in the vegetation from one side to another. They almost certainly notice the change from dense forest to subalpine scrub as they climb up toward Logan Pass and back down, but their reaction to the drive is probably more on the scale (if not the sweeping eloquence) of Thomas Wolfe's, who wrote this during a 1938 visit only five years after the Going-to-the-Sun Road was opened:

> Back again from St. Mary's crossing and the cabins along the Going to the Sun Pass and the stupendous hackled peaks now—the sheer basaltic walls of glaciation, the steep scoopings down below, the dense vortices of glacial valley slopes and forest—and climbing climbing to the Logan Pass so down again terrifically, and the glacial wall beside, the enormous hackled granite peaks before, the green steep glaciation of the forest, the pouring cascades, and the streams below—and down and down the miraculous road into the forest, and by rushing waters, and down and down to the McDonald Lake and Hotel . . .

Mosses, ferns, and a great variety of flowering plants line the streams of Waterton/ Glacier, often growing to a height that obscures the view for hikers and wildlife alike.

Setting aside Wolfe's geology problems (he wouldn't have seen basalt or granite, though he was fairly typical in thinking he did), this vividly describes what impresses most one-day travelers. With all the hackled peaks and miraculous roads, who will notice subtlety?

In Glacier, subtlety is spelled moisture. From the smallest bog to the grandest streamside cottonwoods to the tenacious lichens clinging to the highest crests, moisture is the decisionmaker for what plant life will do.

The one-sentence explanation of Glacier's plant life runs something like "The west side is wetter than the east side, so it has different vegetation." Predictably, the situation is a great deal more involved. To begin with, this explanation gives the impression that the winds coming across the country from the coast hang up on the Continental Divide in Glacier, dump their precipitation on the west side, and have little left for the east side or the prairie beyond. Sounds like a classic rainshadow effect, and it happens, but it isn't all that's going on.

In fact, there isn't much difference in precipitation between the west and east sides. Polebridge, up the valley of the North Fork on the west boundary, and Sherburne Lake, directly across the park on the east boundary, are within a third of an inch of each other in annual precipitation. Farther south, two other opposing villages, West Glacier and East Glacier, are within a half an inch of each other in precipitation. Similar parallels prevail in average temperatures and in relative humidity. So what causes the differences?

One factor is the wind, especially winter wind. While you can count on exceptional, even extraordinary, winds on the peaks anywhere in the park, the east side, including Waterton Lakes National Park to the north, gets some amazing winter winds down through its narrow valleys. They are not always cold (this country being famous for its warm "chinooks" that briefly melt midwinter snows), but they are powerful. St. Mary recorded gusts of one hundred miles per hour in December 1979, as did Many Glacier a year later.

Such winds may damage plants simply by breaking or ripping off their limbs, but they have other effects, too. We think of drought as a hot, dry phenomenon, but it also occurs in the cold, when strong, arid winds dehydrate a tree's branches (a process heightened by strong sunlight). While these violent winds are pummeling every exposed living thing and desiccating soils and plants on the east side, over on the west side things are quiet, especially in winter, when the year's lightest winds pass through.

For a really easy and persuasive look at the effects of these winter winds, take a ride northwest from Babb, up the Chief Mountain International Highway toward the Canadian border. You'll drive for miles through beautiful but very short aspen forests, which stretch across the lower ridges of the foothills of the Rocky Mountain Front. This is a hard place to be an aspen, but apparently the soil is so accommodating that the species thrives in great abundance—grove after grove of gnarled, dwarfish trees with the tiny leaves that characterize aspen

Reynolds Creek dashes from the stunted forests near Logan Pass into progressively more robust plant communities.

MINIATURE FORESTS

Glacier's timberline is a fantasy world of miniature forests. Stunted by extreme winds and frost (the latter working on the roots as well as on the exposed limbs), desiccated by chinook winds and strong sun, the trees take on a "krummholz" or shrublike form, with all their branches pennanted out on the side away from the wind. Some are "flagged krummholz," so named because they've gained enough height that their top, or flag, pokes above the winter snows and is pounded by winter winds. The characteristic shape of this form is a low, full bush with a tuft-topped stalk a few feet high emerging from it. Others are "cushion krummholz," packed low to the ground and often quite dense. Many trees develop "skirts" that reach out around the tree right at ground level. Some bunch together in narrow "islands" around some unusually sturdy individual, whose shade and shelter foster a miniforest, maybe of several species, huddled together for such shared benefits as wind- and temperature-screening and structural reinforcement.

in its most extreme environment. In the fall, when these aspens turn blazing gold, their only rival for photogeneity in the park are the pale yellow larch forests that stretch up and down the North Fork valley and Middle Fork of the Flathead River on the park's opposite boundary.

But wind isn't the only difference between the west side and the east side. Another is elevation. The valleys on the east side tend to be considerably higher than those on the west, and as I described earlier, it doesn't take much change in elevation to make a big change in vegetation. The biggest east-side lake, St. Mary, at 4,484 feet elevation, is significantly higher than its west-side counterpart, McDonald, at 3,153 feet.

And so, yes, the west is different from the east, and Lake McDonald is probably most different of all. Here, low elevation and a moist, moderate climate combine to create a coastal vignette, a Pacific Northwest forest of western hemlock and red cedar. When I walk here along the lake, or up the Avalanche Lake Trail, I am carried in memory to paths along my favorite West Coast salmon rivers. Here along the hushed and damply soft trails of this forest, more than any other forest in the park, I understand why people treasure ancient forests.

Disturbing Scenes

Wild ecosystems are incredibly flexible. The days seem gone when nature was seen as a rigid machine proceeding soldierlike through various stages of growth and plant succession, all of it evolving on a clearly determined course. You don't have to read the new literature of chaos to understand how complex a place like Glacier is—all you have to do is look around. The very sloppiness between the geological layers and the vegetation layers tells the story.

Consider avalanches. When a batch of new rock breaks loose high on a cliff, or some growing imbalance finally puts an existing pile of loose rock beyond its angle of repose, an immediate corporate reorganization is undertaken. The 1968 Slide Lake rockfall avalanche, on the north side of Yellow Mountain (the large, complicated ridge immediately south of Chief Mountain), measured more than a mile from the base of the mountain to where its leading edge came to rest in the channel of Otatso Creek (which it dammed, creating Slide Lake). Upwards of a square mile of the mountain's lower slopes, all the way down to the riparian zone of the creek, were covered to a depth of several yards with new stone. That's habitat alteration at its most dramatic, and it happens frequently on more modest scales all over these mountains.

Snow avalanches make a lot more headlines, probably because they happen more frequently and are more likely to kill some of us. Their effects are also more easily recognized on heavily vegetated landscapes, especially in places where they recur every so often. Avalanche chutes are the contraries of this landscape, going against the grain of both the geological and the vegetation layers that at least roughly follow horizontal contours. You can't miss them. As you hike a trail along the side of a steep slope, you suddenly emerge into a shrubby, treeless expanse, one that runs clear from treeline down to the bottom of the grade.

The scientific literature cautions against interpreting too confidently what has happened in such a place. The vegetation you see is probably not merely what has sprung up since the last avalanche. These chutes tend to favor certain kinds of plants (like really springy ones and those that might survive extended snow burial). These chutes also might host a great variety of snowslides—maybe a big one that sweeps the whole chute one year, then a little one that winds down a central gully the next, each one affecting the vegetation differently.

If you see an obvious avalanche chute, try this: after taking a good look up at what the avalanche did to the landscape as it came down the mountain, turn around and try to figure out what effect it had on the flat country. Sometimes the most impressive effects are at the bottom, or even partway up a slope on the opposite side of the valley; the snow can go a long way uphill on the momentum from such a steep launching.

No less dramatic and a lot more controversial, fire is another great reorganizer of wild landscapes. During the Yellowstone fires of 1988, Americans may not have learned a lot about fire ecology, but they were suddenly a lot more aware that big fires are still a part of our world. Glacier had what by most standards would be regarded as a big fire in 1988, too. The Red Bench fire caused more property damage than any other fire in Montana that year, but at "only" thirty-eight thousand acres it was not noticed by national media, who were more interested in the hundreds of thousands of burned acres in Yellowstone.

The ecological necessity of these wildland fires has become almost a cliché among naturalists interpreting wilderness values. Practically every life community in Glacier evolved to its present form in the presence of fire. Fire shapes and recycles these communities. And all of those variables that influence the geological and vegetative setting come into play after the fire has passed, so that soil, slope, aspect, moisture, wind, and other inorganic processes affect the character of the new community.

Recently, while hiking into a wolf-rendezvous site on the west side of the park (where I happily settled for the sighting of some wolf scat, the wolves being somewhere else), a friend and I passed through a young stand of lodgepole pine. I was shocked to realize that they were six year olds that had come up since the Red Bench fire; shocked because some were as tall as I was, while down in Yellowstone, few six year olds had reached my waist yet. Such are the vicissitudes of soil and moisture from one area to the next.

Preston Park

In late October, a National Biological Service ecologist invited me to join her and some people from a nature conservancy group on a hike up to Preston Park, a cirque reachable by a short steep hike from the Going-to-the-Sun Road a few miles east of Logan Pass. The snow was several inches to a foot deep, so the group "postholed" along, each putting his or her feet in the deep tracks of the person in front. We encountered all the usual wonders along the way: black bear

Matahpi Peak looms over a near-timberline forest that shows the stress of its precarious existence.

prints a day or so old, unforgettable views of the "back" side of the Garden Wall, the looming presence of Matahpi Peak, and, when we stopped near the lake below Siyeh Pass, a long-distance view southwest to Reynolds Mountain. It was all so obviously poised on the edge of winter, all so obviously about to be out of reach, that our enjoyment of it was all the keener.

The ecologist was there to tell us about the park's whitebark pine. She pointed to the large stands of this tough, handsome tree, making sure we noticed how many dry gray snags protruded from the groves. In harsh environments like this, and in any forest where fire is allowed, one expects such snags, so I don't think many of us would have given them much thought. She explained that blister rust, a nonnative disease introduced inadvertently by humans to North America, was gradually killing the whitebark pines. Eventually Glacier National Park could lose almost all of this species. To this audience, made up of people from many disciplines but all aware of the ecological shocks of such a loss, such news was horrifying. Whitebark pine nuts are an important food of grizzly bears and a variety of smaller but equally interesting animals. The loss of this species of tree, beyond its own aesthetic worth, would ripple throughout these high elevations with consequences as grave as they were unpredictable.

Like it or not, humans are a big and very active part of even the wildest of North America's landscapes. Of Glacier's thousand or so species of flowering plants, 13 percent (more than a hundred) are not native; we've added them to this setting in the past century or so. We have not yet lessened the magic of this place, but long before we knew to care about such things we set in motion processes that someday will. For now, this knowledge makes Glacier seem all the more precious.

Hardy grasses and shrubs enjoy the brief Preston Park summer in a wetland that is frozen much of the year.

THE WOLF RETURNS

Among the more troubling legacies of the "Old West" was the destruction of some of the most interesting animals of the wilderness, the predators. Gray wolves were essentially eliminated from the Northern Rockies by the early 1900s, when people believed that the line between good and bad animals was a very simple one. Times change, and so do attitudes. Though quite a few westerners, including many of those in political power, still fear or hate wolves, the vast majority of the American public takes a more tolerant view, and wolf recovery has become a growing concern. Wolves are recolonizing northwestern Montana from Canada. Since the early 1980s, wolves have ranged farther and farther into Montana, and by 1993 there were three packs that included some part of Glacier National Park in their territories. Other packs and individuals have been exploring other areas in Montana, and by 1995 the Montana wolf population had reached perhaps seventy animals.

With the wolves come further changes in public attitudes. Now that they have been around for a decade or so, and dire predictions of massive livestock slaughter and attacks on humans proved to be unfounded, tolerance has increased. Wolf-related gifts, clothing, art, and other items are stocked in stores around the park and the state, and the wolf's symbolic appeal is buttressed by a growing economic power.

In Glacier, the wolf joins many other predator species, all determined to make a living on the available prey species. The wolf has, in fact, wandered into a very busy neighborhood where making a living is hard work. But the wolf has found a place here, one it was banished from long ago. The Glacier country has been healed a little by this colonization of a lost native, and the experience of the park is enriched by its presence.

At dawn one day in late May, as I turned off the highway at Babb and headed up toward Many Glacier, the distant, snowy slopes looked about the same as they had that day at Preston Park, but this was the opposite end of winter. Down south in Yellowstone, the early tourist season was already underway, but here there were no signs of the bustle and society that occupy this road all summer. It was cold, windy, and spitting snow—close to my ideal conditions for watching wildlife. It's not that you have to have bad weather to see animals, but if you do have it, you can count on seeing them by yourself.

Many Glacier is always a great place to look for wildlife, but it was unbelievably generous this day, though every building in the place was still locked up from the winter. A mile east of the development, a mule deer doe stood on a rise above the road in front of me just before I noticed a cow elk farther back on the edge of a small aspen grove. As I passed the lane to the hotel, a white-tailed doe ran across the road in front of me.

At 6:35, I parked in front of the Swiftcurrent motor inn, slipped the spotting scope mount over the car window, and began to scan the slopes in all directions. Right away, I saw a single mountain goat part way up Grinnell Point, the eminence to the south. Ten minutes later, four mule deer came out onto the parking lot and watched me for a while before drifting back into the trees. A minute later, scanning the steep

Red-osier dogwood, white birch, and cedars present a solid front to the casual observer, but offer hospitality to numerous species of birds and mammals.

CROSSED TRAILS
THE COMPLICATIONS OF WILD LIFE

cliffs of Altyn Peak to the north, I saw a second goat, and then a cow elk appeared in the brush just above and behind the motor inn. Scanning to the northwest, I found a herd of eleven bighorn sheep settled in a high ravine, well above the heavy cover; from their position, they had at least some shelter from the wind without having their view blocked in any direction. As I watched them they started to move off in various directions, so I followed the ravine up and up to the cliffs above it, where I picked out two more goats from the goat-sized patches of old snow.

At 6:52, I saw what I was most looking for. A grizzly bear sow became partly visible, moving through the scrubby vegetation only a little ways up the slope behind the motor inn. Over the next few minutes, her two cubs revealed themselves, and then they all settled down in a little grove of mixed brush and aspen and evergreens. Though I followed their movements over the next half hour, I never got as good a look again.

I kept watching through the occasional snow shower, losing my view as curtains of snow and sleet swept across the higher slopes. Then, about 7:30, I drove half a mile or so back to another pullout that allowed me to scan the mountains southeast of Many Glacier. This was where I really appreciated a strong scope, which can bring large mammals three or four miles away up to a recognizable size. I soon picked out a big lumbering form in some high meadows on Wynn Mountain: another grizzly bear, this one probably a big male, judging from its proportions and general massiveness. For about fifteen minutes I watched him wander around with his nose to the ground, grazing or digging or just sniffing for possibilities. Then, fairly well exhilarated with my good fortune at seeing so much activity, I headed back to St. Mary for some coffee and a hot shower. That evening, I returned with my friend Marsha, and to the morning's list of species we added a young bull moose with his antlers in velvet, about halfway between Babb and St. Mary.

Thinking back on that day, it occurred to me that these big mammals had displayed themselves with almost travel brochure perfection. The moose was near the lake, just where moose are supposed to be. Down low, either in riparian areas or lower meadows, were the deer. The elk ranged in and out of the aspen. The bighorn sheep worked their way across the high slopes, never far from the steeper "escape terrain" they depend upon for safety. The goats were above all the others, in their most photogenic habitat of nearly sheer rock walls. Of course, the grizzly bears showed up pretty much anywhere they wanted. It all had the ecological tidiness of a half-hour television nature show, lacking only a supremely confident commentator explaining how nicely all this habitat partitioning works.

And in fact, it does work well. It's hardly that simple in real life, but on the average, that's how these big animals divide up the park, spreading their populations and attentions across the layers and levels of geology and vegetation to the best possible advantage.

GRIZZLY TRAILS

Hiking and camping in grizzly country is different. If you're doing it right, you are always aware that you're not the top carnivore, and that good manners and your own safety require caution. But grizzly country has value besides providing a good scare or convincing hikers to be really tidy around camp. The presence of bears, and your consciousness of it, are keys to tuning in all manner of other things.

The bears' tastes are at least as diverse as yours, and you're going to walk right through the middle of their salad bar. With any luck at all, you'll see some sign of them—tracks, scat, diggings—that connect you to their appetites and urges. That's a benefit, because it sharpens your understanding of large-carnivore conservation. More bears are killed in national parks by the foolishness of people than by any other cause, and it's our responsibility to do right by these priceless animals.

Grizzly country is also a treat on a more esoteric level, as it invites you to participate in a rich and thriving folklore, a near-mythology of nature that humans have constructed around the bear. Every sign of bear offers you a link into that world, whether it stirs your soul or just gives you a laugh. Once at a trailhead I heard some hikers, obviously new to grizzly country, reporting to a ranger on a pile of bear scat they'd found on the trail a few miles away. The ranger calmly answered their questions and agreed with their big-eyed assertions that, yes, sometimes the piles are "really big," but finally had to explain that you can't tell everything about a bear just by seeing a pile of poop. They were a little let down by the failure of this pile to tell them everything they wanted to know, but after a moment's thought, one of them said, "It does, however, answer the age-old question."

Appetites

We North Americans, even those of us with a special interest in nature, tend to see our wild country as inhabited by a small set of animals—nothing like the amazing diversity of Africa or southern Asia. Though we hardly ever say so, we think of our native wildlife as fairly simple: a few species of predators and a few species of prey.

But consider just the mammalian predators in Glacier and Waterton. Starting from the largest, they include grizzly bear, black bear, mountain lion, gray wolf, wolverine, coyote, lynx, bobcat, badger, otter, fisher, striped skunk, mink, marten, long-tailed weasel, short-tailed weasel, least weasel, and a variety of shrews and bats. If the number of different-sized animals is any measure of diversity, this is hardly a depauperate system. Their poundage, in the same order, is 350, 200, 110, 90, 40, 35, 20, 20, 20, 15, 10, 8, 2, 2, and then, from the weasels on down, various fractions of a pound, until we get to the shrews, which are various fractions of an ounce. If that set of numbers doesn't represent a full enough spectrum of ecological niches, keep in mind that a very large and hungry number of birds, fish, reptiles, amphibians, and insects are also out there filling in the gaps. Most of them stay anonymous to the average visitor, but they are not anonymous to one another.

When you think about the incredible number of combinations of predator and prey that exist among all these meat eaters and their even more diverse victims, you begin to doubt that the term "food web" does justice to the richness of what's going on out there. It's more like a food tapestry, or a food Persian rug. A large part of what is consumable is of interest to a large percentage of the consumers, who often seem limited only by how big a piece of food they can fit in their mouths. If it's too big to kill, they'll wait until something else kills it and then sneak up to the carcass for a quick snack. On the other hand, almost all of them, from the largest grizzly bear to the smallest shrew, eat insects. These in turn chew or bite or otherwise live off the mammals, whether alive or dead. Studies elsewhere in the Rockies have revealed that several dozen species of highly specialized beetles make their entire living off large mammal carcasses; some of these beetles are so specialized they prey only on other beetles that scavenge only these carcasses. Considering all the larger scavengers and the amazing number of invertebrates and smaller animals who help clean up a carcass, a dead elk is itself a very complex ecosystem.

We've learned a lot about how these large mammals interact, and what we've learned is that life is hard. Between 1989 and 1994, thirty-two deer, twenty-three elk, and twelve moose, all females, were radio-collared in and near the park on the North Fork Flathead River. Of these sixty-seven ungulates, mountain lions killed ten deer and eleven elk. Wolves killed eight deer, three elk, and four moose. Bears killed two deer, three elk, and three moose. Coyotes killed four deer. Humans killed four deer, five elk, and two moose. Three deer, one elk, and two moose died of unknown causes, and one moose died of an accident. Only one of the sixty-seven radio-collared animals, a deer, was known to have died of old age.

T*he forests and slopes of the Avalanche Creek drainage are home to an enormous variety of wildlife, from the dippers and ducks on the lake to the squirrels and martens in the trees and the deer and bears who roam the forest floor.*

Predators' appetites know no professional courtesy, either; they'll eagerly eat one another or one another's food. Wolf researchers recently discovered the remains of a mountain lion kitten that had been caught and killed by wolves and have documented wolves taking lions' kills away from them. A more recent addition to the local carnivore lore is a grizzly bear in northwestern Glacier National Park who spends part of its winter out of its den making a comfortable living by chasing wolves away from their fresh kills. Opportunism is the word of the day.

Bull

The farthest north, and most remote, of the long, narrow lakes up the west side of the park is Kintla. When you look north from Kintla Lake, you see Starvation Ridge and the Boundary Mountains and know that Canada is on the other side. The trail follows the north shore of the lake for six or seven miles, sometimes winding perversely away from the lake shore and up over a steep hill, as if the trail crew had decided that hikers should have to suffer a little to enjoy such a wonderful view.

An old friend, a resource-management biologist in Glacier, has been my companion on several recent hikes, including a late-fall trip up the Kintla drainage, past Kintla Lake to its smaller sister, Upper Kintla. I was here especially to get a look at a bull trout, which spawn in small numbers in a nearby creek. A seasonal biological technician with the National Park Service was camped and was good enough to take these unannounced guests to the best spot. As it happened, the best spot was on the other side, so our host loaned me his waders. I eased across the channel, climbed up on a gravel bar, put on my polaroids, and squinted into the bright water.

After a minute or two, I was able to pick out the shapes of several big trout, up to eighteen or twenty inches, as they moved slowly here and there in the deepest part of the pool. Their profiles were flattened by refraction, but there was no doubt of what they were. The leading edges of their pectoral and pelvic fins were so white they almost glowed. Like their near-relatives, the brook and lake trout, bull trout have very pretty, multicolored underfins. I watch fish the way many people watch birds, so this was a pretty satisfying moment.

The bull trout is a convenient symbol for much of what has happened to wild western aquatic ecosystems. It is illegal to kill bull trout in the park, and Upper Kintla Lake contains the last large population that has not had any nonnative fishes dumped on top of it. Elsewhere in the bull trout's range, introduced lake trout have hammered it, introduced brook trout have confused its genetics by breeding with it, and introduced fishermen have overharvested it.

National parks, for all the damage they have sustained, are now viewed as among the last strongholds of some rare native fishes such as the bull trout. Like many Western

Lost Lake's name carries a light irony, for the lake's roadside location would make it seem impossible to lose, but most visitors hurry by without noticing or taking a moment to enjoy the reflection of Little Chief Mountain.

United States waters, Glacier's lakes and streams were subjected to heavy stocking of a variety of nonnative sport fish, six species of which took hold and now dominate many waters. Many fishless high-country lakes and ponds, representing unique aquatic plant and invertebrate communities, were arduously stocked by pack trains in the interest of improving the fishing for early visitors. The inadvertent result was the destruction or irrevocable alteration of whatever biological system had developed in those waters over the past ten thousand years. By the time all stocking ceased in 1972, massive changes had been inflicted on the native aquatic world here.

But for all that, Glacier's waters are still important reservoirs of native fishes. Besides protecting bull trout, the park remains one of the last strongholds of lake populations of westslope cutthroat trout. Almost everywhere else, introductions of rainbow, brown, and even other types of cutthroats have outcompeted the native westslope cutthroats. We only faintly understand what we set in motion when we tinker with these systems; in the end our actions almost always bite back.

T
he bugling of bull elk is one of the characteristic sounds of remote western wilderness. The bugle may echo for miles from the high peaks, a challenge to other bulls and an unwitting call to large predators who sometimes prey on the distracted, battle-weary bulls.

The Eagle and the Shrimp

Perhaps the best example of the twisted course of such aquatic tinkering is the story of the kokanee salmon of McDonald Creek. It is the kind of story that chills the hearts and heats the conversations of all of us who seek to understand just what national parks offer us and how they should be managed. Ultimately it is not a story of fish but of the entire ecosystem and how one unconsidered action echoes through it forever.

Kokanee salmon, a landlocked version of the sockeye salmon, were first introduced into Flathead Lake, southwest of the park, in 1916. They soon replaced the native westslope cutthroat, and by the 1930s, they found their way up the Flathead River to the park, where they discovered excellent spawning habitat in McDonald Creek, just below McDonald Lake. Here they spawned by the thousands, and, like all Pacific salmon, died as soon as they were done.

Scavengers noticed this right away. In 1939, 37 bald eagles were counted along this little stretch of water, and that number grew to what has been called "the densest concentration of the species south of Canada." In 1981, when more than a hundred thousand kokanee entered the stream to spawn, 639 eagles were counted on a single day. People flocked to see them. Down in Wyoming and southern Montana, all through the 1970s and 1980s, I heard about this eagle show, and I always meant to go see it. I shouldn't have waited.

Starting in the late 1960s, the state of Montana introduced a nonnative crustacean, opossum shrimp, into some lakes in the upper Flathead River valley. The idea was that these shrimp would serve as a food that would accelerate the growth of sport fish. By 1981, the shrimp had been washed downstream to Flathead Lake, and something went spectacularly wrong. The kokanee population collapsed with incredible swiftness. In 1987, only 330 kokanee

T*he black bears of Glacier are master adapters, fitting them- selves into a busy predator-prey system with a flexibility and ingenuity that leads them to abundant food while keeping them out of the way of grizzly bears, wolves, and mountain lions.*

entered McDonald Creek, and in 1989 only 50 showed up. The eagles didn't hang around to see what humans would come up with next, and the show was over.

Biologists are still sorting out what happened. They know, for example, that the kokanee were unable to feed on the shrimp because the two species lived at different depths in Flathead Lake and didn't run into each other much. They also know that both the shrimp and the kokanee feed heavily on a variety of lake zooplankton, microscopic animals whose abundance dramatically declined shortly after the shrimp arrived. The shrimp may have simply outcompeted the kokanee for this food source. Biologists suspect that increased growth of lake trout, whose juveniles were able to feed heavily on the shrimp, may have given lake trout an edge in their competition with the kokanee. Lake trout also prey on kokanee, so the more lake trout, the fewer kokanee.

There are engaging ironies in the disappointment this all caused. Here was a national park with a terrific wildlife attraction: not only a sensational salmon run but also a remarkable gathering of predators and scavengers, including eagles, bears, coyotes, otters, mink, gulls, and ducks. But the whole thing was based on the intrusion into the ecosystem of a nonnative animal, an introduced fish. By almost any of the prevailing definitions of national parks, the show was "unnatural." But it was also wildly popular, and among the Glacier visitors and locals who reminisce about it, one rarely hears any sentiments of relief that the native ecosystem has been to some extent restored. And considering our ongoing concern about the well-being of many of those predators and scavengers, it's easy to regret this loss, however artificial its circumstances. The park's "unnatural" situation was without question benefiting the regional bald eagle population, and that has to have been a good thing. Nobody ever said managing national parks was going to be simple.

The Scattered System

I am most often attracted to the fauna of Glacier National Park—62 mammal species, 273 birds, 23 fish, 40 mollusks, 9 reptiles and amphibians, 102 butterflies, 200 spiders, 2,000 beetles, and so on—for the fun and wonder of the individual, whether it be a spruce grouse along a trail or a cow elk in a riverbend clearing. But the fauna are the part of the setting here that teach us the most as populations, too. They teach us about the extraordinary reach of this place and the equally extraordinary vulnerability of it all.

In the summer of 1983, I visited Glacier to interview then-superintendent Bob Haraden as part of an assignment for *Newsweek*. During our conversation, he summed up both the power and the powerlessness of trying to manage and protect a place that is so connected to the lands around it: "There are damages we can stop, problems that, if we had enough rangers to line them up at arm's length all along the boundary, we could solve. But even if the rangers were twelve deep they couldn't stop the acid rain from falling."

FOLLOWING PAGES: From the shores of Lake Sherburne, the entire range of large-mammal habitats in Glacier are visible, from the lowlands inhabited by deer, elk, and moose (and once bison) to the high homes of bighorn sheep and goats and the distant ridges of Mount Allen.

What we have learned, in our 120 or so years of experimenting with national parks, is that the boundaries don't work very well. They might be fine for the American marten, with its tiny home range. They might even be fine for most of the park's animals and plants. Glacier will continue to be a breathtaking, glorious place no matter what care we take of its neighboring lands. But it's good not to forget what is at stake, and a few examples should serve to make the point that Glacier is no more an island than any place else on the planet. As an ecologist friend of mine puts it, "ecosystems leak."

Modern conservationists have concentrated on protecting the "Crown of the Continent" Ecosystem, which includes Glacier and Waterton Lakes National Parks, the Bob Marshall-Great Bear-Scapegoat Wilderness complex to the south, and various other bordering lands, many of which are already intensively developed and others that are targeted for development. For campaigns to save the grizzly bear and some other species, that is where the boundary is drawn. But to explain where Glacier really fits in things, I must go well beyond that and celebrate a far larger ecosystem.

Some of it is already gone. Bison once ranged the low country on the east side (I suppose some were on the west side, too), and early accounts talk of many bison bones and skulls found in the lower valleys of the park. We don't know exactly where or when those herds moved; some may have wintered in the more sheltered valleys in the park, while others may have moved long distances as part of the migratory tides of the great herds of the northern plains. By their migrations, they defined a much larger ecosystem, one that tied the mountains to the prairies. Caribou apparently also once inhabited portions of the northwestern corner of the park, and perhaps other parts of the park, too. They're gone, and their migrations no longer enrich the ecological interconnections of this region.

But many other such wild travelers are still around and have the power to surprise us. A most unlikely and important migrant is the army cutworm moth. From mid- to late-summer, all up and down the mountain ranges in and near Glacier, some grizzly bears move to high-elevation talus slopes to eat these little moths. At their peak condition, these insects are more than half fat and almost a calorie each. They are superabundant, and heavy concentrations of them may hold bears in one area for several weeks. The exact natural history of the local moths is still being sorted out, but they are known to migrate seasonally over very long distances to and from prairie habitats. In other places they may go hundreds of miles. Glacier's moths may move well beyond anybody's definition of the ecosystem, but they are very important to the bears.

Longer-distance fliers include the bald eagles that stopped over at McDonald Creek back when the kokanee were so abundant. Those birds were moving along a two-thousand-mile migration flyway that extends from their summering areas in the Mackenzie

This flower-fringed marsh near Camas Creek is a likely place to find moose.

Left: **Mule deer are common residents of the park's many valleys and are frequently seen even in the major park developments.**

Left: **The bushy-tailed Columbian ground squirrel is one of Glacier's more versatile herbivores, at home in the low country as well as near the high passes.**

Thimbleberry, with its broad leaves reminiscent of maples and soft reddish berries, is common in avalanche chutes, where it is a popular food for animals ranging from small birds to big bears.

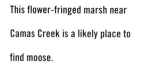

of the wonder of life in Glacier & Waterton. Climb from the lowest elevation to the highest and you will see that the zones do not have clear boundaries; in fact, life exists here in a continuum, not in tidy bands of different communities.

Plants that we consider characterisitic of one zone straggle up and down the trail above and below that zone. Animals move all over the place, so that ground squirrels scurry around near the high passes as well as in the prairie grasses, and mountain goats may make their way from their famous high haunts to the river bottoms now and then, especially if they know of a good mineral lick down there.

But for all the diffuse interaction of life communities on the slopes of these mountains, the life-zone concept is an important key to understanding. Most of the time, most places, it's easy to tell which zone you are in. There's no mistaking prairie meadow, or krummholz, or least of all the highest crags of raw rock. There's also no mistaking the preferred habitats of the larger ani-

mals. The mammals drift up and down this landscape rather like the snowline that some of them follow in their search for food; the grazers seek forage at its peak of nutrition, and the predators seek the grazers. But each species does so in a manner that is, if observed long and carefully enough, predictable and sensible.

The arrangement of homes and food supplies and appetites is no accident here, but the result of thousands of years of sorting out the possibilities, as all these separate but connected lives find their ways.

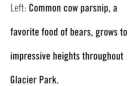

Left: **Common cow parsnip, a favorite food of bears, grows to impressive heights throughout Glacier Park.**

Glacier's fir forests are home to many of the park's large mammals, as well as a variety of the smaller "fur bearers," including American marten, fisher, the weasels, wolverine, and porcupine.

Left: **You may hear the sharp whistling alarm call of hoary marmots before you see them, but their preference for large rocks as lookout posts makes them easy to spot.**

River basin of far northern Canada to wintering areas in the United States as far south as southern Utah.

Less understood but no less significant are all the little neotropical migrants: songbirds that summer in the northern Rockies and winter in Central and South America, several thousand miles away. These, even more than the moths and eagles, are in grave danger. Their seasonal habitats are being destroyed in places that Bob Haraden's line of rangers may never have heard of. Glacier National Park is really only part of a vast and unappreciated Western Hemisphere Ecosystem, and it can only retain its ecological integrity if the rest of the planet does.

Communities of life—like the moss that carpets this rock wall—thrive in the least hospitable of places.

LIFE ZONES: FINDING A WAY

The cynical chaotician in Michael Crichton's science fiction thriller *Jurassic Park* said it all when he observed that "life finds a way." Life's capacity to spread and make itself at home is the defining characteristic of the biosphere. Given only oxygen, the slightest source of nourishment, and some little thing to hold onto, life appears in the most improbable places, from miles deep in the oceans to the highest peaks and beyond. Glacier & Waterton provides a relatively undisturbed stage for life to exercise its adaptation skills, and thus provides us with front row seats for the show.

It is a show in several acts, which we have chosen to call "life zones." These zones are draped horizontally across the landscape, following roughly the same contours as the geological layers underneath them. From the lowest prairie communities on the east side, adapted to very low rainfall, to the highest bare-rock, sheer-walled peaks where only the occasional lichen and other hardy life survive, life finds a way.

The life-zone concept is convenient and, if used carefully, true to the reality you find when you climb from the prairie to the high passes, but its appreciation requires a certain tolerance for imprecision. Cross the park west to east and you will find striking changes in the placement of the zones as moisture regime and prevailing winds change. Circle a single mountain from one side to the other and you may find the zones shifting downward or upward hundreds of feet in response to exposure to sunlight or wind. Climb in and out of a deep ravine and you may find remarkably different life communities on one side or the other, depending upon its exposure. In fact, such looseness is part

ft: Moss campion, one of the most

iking alpine flowers, has densely

erlaced growth—a tight

ushion" of leaves and branches—

ich helps hold warmth in a

rsh environment.

Right: **Bighorn sheep rarely stray far from the security of steep cliffs, but they are much more likely to graze the gentler lower slopes of Glacier's mountains than are mountain goats.**

Above: **Fireweed follows major disturbances, from road construction to fire and other natural events. The plant flourishes for a few years, then is replaced by other species.**

Aspen, especially common along the east boundary of the park and in the lowlands of the St. Mary and Swiftcurrent valleys, attract elk, deer, beaver, bears, and a variety of smaller mammals and birds.

Above: **Blue grouse are often met on the trails throughout the park. Give one a patient audience and it may reveal the presence of several more, with whom it joins in soft conversation.**

*B*ighorn rams use
their heavy horns
against each other in
spectacular collisions
and less decisive
shoving matches. In
order to survive the
torque and impact of
these battles, bighorn
sheep have evolved
skulls, as well as neck
muscles and vertebrae,
that cushion the blow.

*T*hough death is a
normal part of the
wilderness process,
humans have
accelerated the death
rate of the whitebark
pine in Glacier by
introducing disease.

Morning
mist burns off
Loon Lake.

Moose frequent
many park wetlands,
lakes, and streams,
where they are comfort-
able wading shoulder-
deep and more in
search of succulent
aquatic plants. For all
their size and power,
moose are still preyed
upon effectively by
wolves and bears.

FOLLOWING PAGES:
Goat Mountain is
reflected in a pond
at dawn.

I prefer to approach Glacier from the east. Driving across the high plains toward the front range, I find myself anxious to clear the final ridge that stands between me and my first glimpse of Chief Mountain. Glacier National Park shares this singular eminence with the Blackfeet Indian Reservation. Chief Mountain is a freestanding outlier of the great Lewis Overthrust, rising alone and imposing against the skyline near the Canadian border. More important, it is a place of spiritual power. Nearly all the tribes and groups of American Indians who have had any contact with the region consider it so, whether as a shrine or a vision-questing site, and for more than two hundred years white travelers have noted it in their journals and books as a great landmark.

Chief Mountain seems to dominate the landscape and attract the eye from whatever direction it is visible, and it is visible for a very long distance. To the east, when I'm out on the reservation and up to the bottom of my heart in a trout lake, I seem always aware of it. Though I may be straining excitedly to cast far enough to reach the heavy rainbows that are slashing at emerging caddisflies, my sight is still drawn to the northwest and the mountain. To the west, skirting Cosley Lake on the trail to the Belly River Ranger Station, I anticipate and then enjoy its emergence from behind Cosley Ridge. And on any road along or out from the east side of the park, I orient myself by it, casually but irresistibly checking to see if it's where I expect it to be on the horizon.

Chief Mountain, a lone sentinel along the park's northeast border with the Blackfeet Reservation, has been a landmark and place of power for people of many cultures.

GLACIER GHOSTS

THE TEN-THOUSAND-YEAR ADVENTURE

Often it isn't quite where I thought, and I realign my mental compass, puzzling over how I got turned around.

It took me a while to realize that I wasn't attracted to this mountain just out of respect for other peoples' spiritual attachment to it or out of interest in its more recent historical significance. It didn't matter what I knew or what spiritual tradition I was part of. This mountain commanded my attention and haunted my thoughts just because it was that kind of place. Its power is not confined to any culture or time, but is something that might be felt by anyone.

Chief Mountain reminds us of a fundamental fact of the Glacier & Waterton area: it may be authentic and uncompromising wilderness, but it is also a cultural landscape, preserving in its remote valleys ten thousand years of human history. After so many years of human occupation, and so much opinion, belief, and folklore growing up around the features of this country, there is no clean separation between culture and nature. We are drawn to places like this as much for the shared human experience of them as for the wonder of their beauty or the challenging fascination of their relatively whole ecological processes.

For better or worse, my culture has given me a great interest in discovery. I like to know who found a place, what they thought of it, and how they named it, especially a place as wonderful as Glacier Park. But the written record tends to emphasize what the Euro-Americans did and thought. The Indians who were here for several hundred generations didn't leave their story in the nice tidy written records left by the parade of early white travelers, so it's easy to overlook them in favor of the Fidlers, DeSmets, Pallisers, Grinnells, Pumpellys, and all the others I can connect with just by going to a good library.

Still, I try to balance my passion for history with a like passion for personal impression. I will never experience Glacier the way an ancient Indian (or a modern one, for that matter) or a Victorian geologist did, and I don't need to. It helps me to know how they saw and used the place, but it's up to me to get what I can from it.

Menus

The road to Waterton Townsite and into the park crosses the Waterton River just below Lower Waterton Lake and along the edge of Maskinonge Lake. Not far from here, where the river emerges from the steep country and sets out across the prairie, is a place that was once a large wintering campsite for native people whose sense of the seasons was far more sophisticated than mine. While I am unable to catch even one pike from Maskinonge Lake, these folks often spent part of their year here, fishing and hunting successfully enough to prosper. We know from archaeological work here that their prey included ungulates (deer, sheep, elk, moose, bison) who came here to winter, as well as a variety of fur bearers (beaver, fox, wolf, coyote), quite a few species of birds (swans, ducks, and geese), and, of course, fish. As spring and summer came, the people followed the animals into higher country.

Place names are sometimes among the oddest cultural attachments of Glacier & Waterton. Vimy Peak, shown here beyond Middle Waterton Lake, was named for Vimy Ridge, the French site of a World War I battle in which Canadian forces played a key role.

*S*t. Mary Lake hosted
the fishermen and
travelers of many
cultures long before it
even received its
modern name or
became a primary
photographic target
of park visitors.

*A*pikuni Mountain,
near Many Glacier,
combined two cultures
in its name. The
moniker was first given
to James Willard Schultz
by his Blackfeet friends,
and then applied to the
mountain in Schultz's
honor by a white friend.

The steep-sided Prince of Wales Hotel, overlooking Waterton Lakes, seems like an architectural answer to the surrounding mountains. The grand old hotels of Waterton and Glacier are a powerful reminder of the older and more genteel traditions of national parks.

Archeologists have established that these seasonal movements were quite complicated and not even consistent from year to year. The people of this region were resourceful rather than habitual. The Glacier/Waterton area was part of a complex set of opportunities that were exploited as need be, perhaps every year, perhaps every few years. When these people found conditions not to their liking, they drew upon a vast store of regional knowledge and adapted.

Today, when I sit in the charming dining room of the Prince of Wales Hotel overlooking Waterton Townsite, I do my foraging less directly, through the dinner menu and the wine list. Gawking at the spectacular view of Upper Waterton Lake, I am supremely comfortable even though my own migration patterns are far more erratic and inscrutable than those of earlier people.

But that is not to slight my culture's own traditions. White people have only been here a couple of hundred years, but this land has shaped our ways, too. I prefer the wilderness parts of the great western parks, but I regularly force myself (this gets easier as I get older) to participate in the most intensely social traditions of these places (such as expensive dinners and clean sheets in nice hotels), if only to remind myself about where these modern parks came from. Glacier, Yellowstone, and most of the other western parks originated in a fairly high-brow touristic tradition considerably older and more politically influential than their current backpacking tradition. These hotels may seem inappropriate to modern wilderness enthusiasts, but they were central to the park experience for many generations. Many if not most visitors to Glacier seventy years ago came to the boundary developments, from which they were launched in long, luxurious pack trains into the high country. The accounts written by these people suggest that one of the things they most enjoyed about the experience was the contrast: into the wild forest for the day, but back to the refreshing antidote of resort life for a good dinner each night.

Familiar Trails

And so I conduct my exploration in two ways. The first adventure is my own, out there along the trails. The second adventure is vicarious, appreciating this place through the eyes and words of those who knew it earlier and better than I ever will. Of course these are both part of the same adventure, the one we all share here.

Archaeologists' reports, though often technical and scientifically conservative (lacking the satisfying conjecture and literary warmth that researchers abhor), are all I need to picture some of the realities of these long-passed families and their ways. Historians' overviews are helpful sometimes, but I'm far more attracted to firsthand accounts; reading along in some early travel book or journal (recoiling from a sudden blast of racism or other ignorance), I make their discoveries again, along with some new ones.

GOING-TO-THE-SUN ROAD

Fall in Glacier brings color to the aspen and a first dusting of snow to the upper slopes of Little Chief Mountain.

(even frightened) millions of visitors since. It turned Glacier from a park with border developments into a place that the average tourist could cross. Until this road over Logan Pass was opened, the only way to experience the high passes or the steep slopes of the mountains was on foot or horseback. All at once, anyone with a car or a bus ticket could do the trip in a couple hours, with stops along the way for assorted wonders and an unrelieved series of stunning vistas. Perhaps if we had it to do over again today we might

For all the grandeur and photogeneity of the hotels of Waterton and Glacier, they are not the most impressive human landmark. That honor almost certainly belongs to a site that was placed on the National Register in 1983 and has the odd dimensions of thirty feet by almost fifty miles. Born in a time when extraordinary engineering projects seemed an appropriate feature of national parks, Going-to-the-Sun Road was dedicated in July 1933 and has thrilled

not do it at all, but this road is now a treasured cultural resource, and so far, at least, movements to widen it and change it from an authentic auto trail into a modern highway have been held off. The road is one of those peculiar elements of some wilderness parks: a human achievement so distinguished and special that it becomes a significant part of the park experience.

Recently, while engaged in this kind of intellectual foraging at the wonderful special collections library at Montana State University, I happened upon a small self-published book by Henry Klussman, *A Trip to the Northwest by Automobile*. On page forty-five I noticed a nice photograph of Gunsight Lake, taken from halfway up the trail to Gunsight Pass. But Klussman's Gunsight Lake of 1922 was different than the one I described in the first chapter. The shoreline I fished was lined with vegetation, but in the photograph, it was lined with the buildings of a chalet, one of seven rustic backcountry Shangri-las that served riding and hiking tourists at the time. It's fashionable to consider the parks overdeveloped these days, and they are struggling with ever larger crowds and pressures, but in some ways they're probably less developed than they were half a century ago. Only two of those seven chalets remain, and one of the reasons I treasure their survival is that they connect me to something that was once important, even precious, in my own culture.

Everywhere I turn in Waterton and Glacier, I encounter my predecessors. Kintla Lakes, where I went to see the bull trout, was the site of one of the first oil wells in Montana more than a century ago. Almost as long ago near Many Glacier, where I recently watched goats and grizzlies in almost complete solitude, a thousand people lived in the mining town of Altyn. Driving any of the roads, I meet a parade of named peaks, lakes, streams, and living things, each humanizing the landscape just a little. And of course in every drainage, no matter how remote, the archaeologist's eye might discern traces of the original human inhabitants of this country, some of whose ancestors still live nearby and hold to their own sense of the land's worth and power. When you travel here, you can enjoy being alone, or you can shift mental gears just a little and share the good company of ten thousand years of common experience.

Taking It Personally

Personally, the only kinds of crowds I have much tolerance for are those spiritual ones. I'd rather hike with a thousand ghosts than share a hotel restaurant with a dozen real live people. The developed areas of the park, for all their huckleberry milkshakes and other amenities, oppress me pretty quickly. Lines of cars creeping along the roads make me grumpy. Even when I'm out in some isolated place with a spotting scope or a fly rod or a backpack, I flinch a little when I hear voices approaching. It has often occurred to me that my aversion to society is nearly bizarre, considering that as a writer I not only need all those people as an audience but I am celebrating (and therefore promoting) the very places I enjoy most when I have them to myself.

I didn't have the parking lot at Logan Pass to myself on a darkly overcast fall day, with lowering clouds driven hard by a winterlike west wind. But as people spilled noisily from cars and vans, I focused on the distance and picked a fast-flying eastbound eagle out of the confusion of grayish sky and snow-patched peaks. The bird's velocity was unbelievable;

False hellebore, with its broad, deeply veined leaves, looks like a transplant from some more tropical setting, but it thrives in moist sites all the way up to the alpine.

outrunning the wind, it crossed over the divide above us and seemed to fast-forward to the east, shrinking smaller and smaller until I lost it in the cross-hatched snow patterns of Heavy Runner Mountain. It was a moment just between me and the eagle, yet shared with a few others in the group, yet entirely missed by others who didn't happen to be paying attention right then. Those of us who saw it didn't say a word to each other, and what could we possibly say to the ones who missed it?

It was not a moment for a camera or quantifying field notes, not something that would advance science or yield to analysis. It was instead the connection we are, after all, out there seeking, when the door opens for an instant on some greater truth, the kind of wisdom that eludes us as soon as we try to turn it into words—its only real value is as untranslated experience. Go to Glacier with your heart open for that, and everything else it has to offer will be yours as well.

Near the head of St. Mary Lake, Virginia Creek drops from its long hanging valley in a series of falls and cascades easily reached from the Going-to-the-Sun Road.

FOLLOWING PAGES:

The first light of morning glows on the pinnacled ridge of Little Chief Mountain, then begins its descent into the darkened cirque below.

ACKNOWLEDGMENTS

I am grateful to the staffs of the Montana State University Library and the Yellowstone Research Library, and especially to Beth Dunagan at the Glacier Park Library, for repeated assistance in tracking down important or obscure material. Rick Balkin provided his usual calm professional guidance, and everyone at Tehabi was a delight to work with. Many other people helped with logistical support, information, advice, snacks, company on the trail, or by reading the manuscript. I must especially thank Wendy Baylor, Steve Frye, Steve Gniadek, Brace Hayden, Mark Johnson, Marsha Karle, Kate Kendall, Leo Marnell, Sean Meegan, Gary Moses, Alex Philp, Jeremy Schmidt, Susan Sindt, and Amy Vanderbilt. Larry Eddy of Painted Sky Llama Ranch introduced me to his endlessly patient and vastly entertaining animals. It was a special treat to hike the Highline Trail with Jeff and Melissa Garton, and a privilege to complement Jeff's superb photography with my text.

PAUL SCHULLERY
Yellowstone, Wyoming

I would like to thank my wife, Melissa, not only for her companionship on the trail but also for her patience as I wrestled with the details of making an image. It was a great pleasure to work with Paul Schullery, a delightful man of wisdom and subtle humor who possesses great command of his craft. It is also a joy to work with the people of Tehabi Books who truly know the meaning of the word Tehabi—many thanks to Tom, Sharon, Sam, Andy, Nancy, and Chris.

JEFF GARTON
Tucson, Arizona

Its peaks and forests still a vital wellspring of inspiration for millions of visitors from around the world, the Glacier landscape fades to silhouette in the gloaming.

INDEX

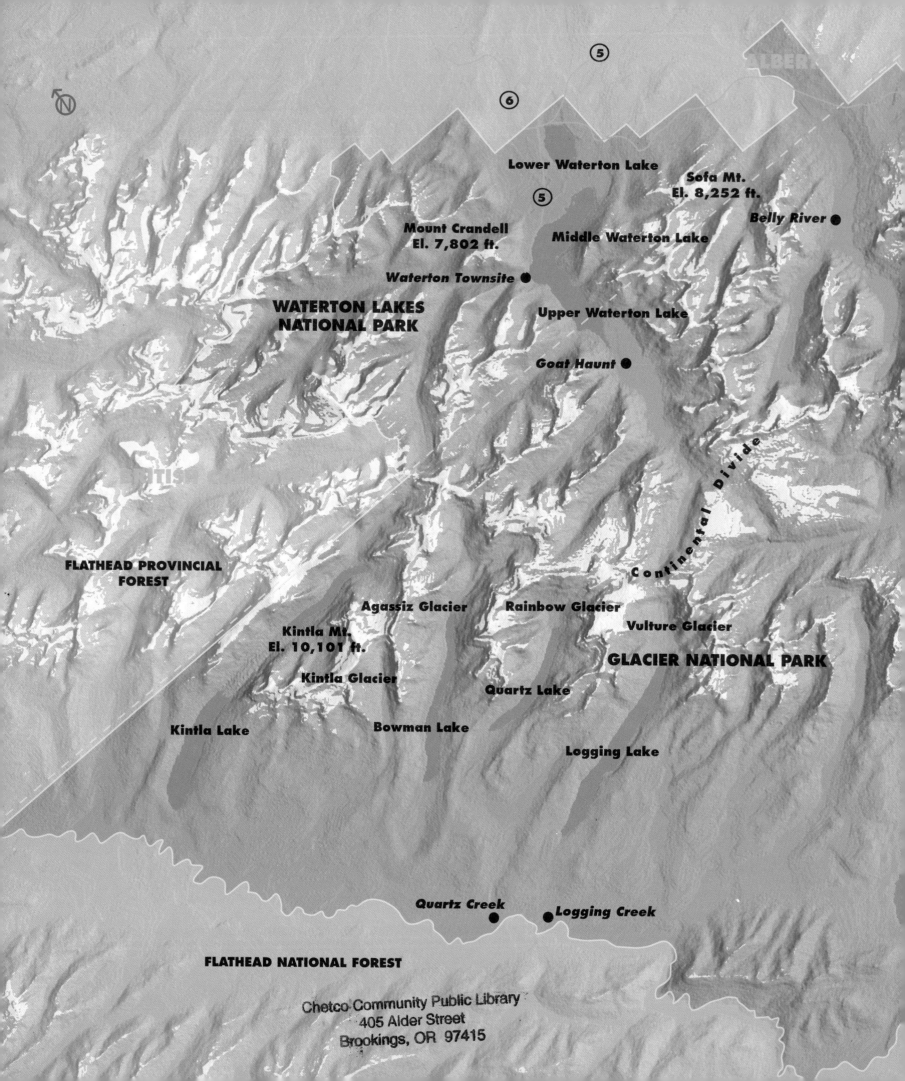

⑤

⑥

Lower Waterton Lake

Sofa Mt.
El. 8,252 ft.

⑤

Belly River ●

Mount Crandell
El. 7,802 ft.

Middle Waterton Lake

Waterton Townsite ●

WATERTON LAKES
NATIONAL PARK

Upper Waterton Lake

Goat Haunt ●

Continental   Divide

FLATHEAD PROVINCIAL
FOREST

Continental Divide

Agassiz Glacier

Rainbow Glacier

Vulture Glacier

Kintla Mt.
El. 10,101 ft.

GLACIER NATIONAL PARK

Kintla Glacier

Quartz Lake

Kintla Lake

Bowman Lake

Logging Lake

Quartz Creek ●   ● **Logging Creek**

FLATHEAD NATIONAL FOREST

Chetco Community Public Library
405 Alder Street
Brookings, OR 97415